''I was born to sing gospel music.''

—Mahalia Jackson, 1954

Mahalia Jackson
Born to Sing Gospel Music

Mahalia Jackson was a magnificent talent with her spellbinding contralto voice. She was deeply religious with a quest to help the underprivileged and the disadvantaged.

"Blues are the songs of despair," Mahalia often said. "Gospel songs belong to the Lord. Gospel songs are the songs of hope. When you sing gospel you have the feeling there is a cure for what's wrong, but when you are through with the blues you've got nothing to rest on."

Before each performance or recording session, Mahalia would sit quietly alone. In describing this time, she said, "I read selected passages from my Bible in order to gather to myself the inner strength I need." Her favorite Biblical quotation was "Make a joyful noise unto God, all ye lands" from Psalm 66. Mahalia saw this Psalm as her mission in life.

It was a mission that required a long, hard climb. But it was a mission she accomplished with enthusiasm. During the years of struggle, Mahalia became an internationally known recording artist and church performer.

However, Mahalia never forgot her humble beginnings. Her mother died when she was six and she was reared by a religious aunt who introduced her "to the joy and passion, sweetness and beauty of the Lord's hymns and anthems." Her father did not feel he could raise the six children alone. He preached on Sunday and doubled as a longshoreman and barber on week days. His time was taken with work. His income was low.

Mahalia never finished school, dropping out in the eighth grade to help make a living by cooking and washing clothes.

Even from her early days, Mahalia carried her gospel message in hundreds of performances. Her involvement in the songs she sang often moved listeners to dance in the aisles.

Mahalia had a prime goal in her life: ''I have hopes that my singing will break down the wall of hate and fear that divides the white and black people of this land.''

Through her magnificent talent Mahalia left a legacy that will continue to bring people to the Lord.

Mahalia Jackson

Born To Sing Gospel Music

by

Evelyn Witter

Illustrated by **Jan Jones**
Cover by **A. G. Smith**

Louise Rock, Editor

LIBRARY OF CONGRESS CATALOGING IN PUBLICATION DATA

Witter, Evelyn
    Mahalia Jackson: Born to Sing Gospel Music

    (The Sowers)
    Bibliography: p. 129
    Includes index.

    SUMMARY: A biography of the renowned gospel singer who hoped, through her art, to break down some of the barriers between black and white people.
    1. Jackson, Mahalia, 1911-1972—Juvenile literature. 2. Gospel musicians—United States—Biography—Juvenile literature. [1. Jackson, Mahalia, 1911-1972. 2. Singers. 3. Afro-Americans—Biography] I. Jones, Jan M., 1949-   illus. II. Smith, A. G. (Alfred Gray) III. Title. IV. Series: Sowers Series.

ML3930.J2W57 1985   783.7'092'4 [B] [92]   85-63234
ISBN 0-88062-045-5 Paperbound

CONTENTS

Mahalia Listened

"We got some crabs and shrimps!" Peter Jackson shouted from his place at the fire on the levee.

Four-year-old Mahalia, his sister, heard him but went right on skipping happily along Water Street in New Orleans. She wanted to hurry to the corner to see the jazz band she could hear in the distance. She wanted to be ready when they turned the corner where she could hear them more plainly. They were probably coming back from a funeral.

Mahalia liked jazz music. But then all sounds interested her. She liked to hear the robins sing. She liked the songs of the red and green birds who made their homes along the river. The shouts of the fishermen on the levee and the cries of the washerwomen and the older boys on the streets were all sounds that made rhythms in the little girl's mind.

As Mahalia stood at the corner listening to the band go by, the woodpeckers kept the beat and the crickets sang in chorus.

It was all a familiar sight where the Jacksons lived in their little three-room house along with the other shacks of poor Negroes, Italians, Creoles, and French. The shacks stretched along the street between the railroad tracks and the Mississippi River. Mahalia did not mind living among the shacks on Water Street. After all, she was born here on October 26, 1911, and knew no other place.

As the band passed on down the street, Mahalia climbed the grassy bank to join her brother, who was still with a group of children up on the levee. They had started a driftwood fire despite the threat of a storm moving toward them from the gulf, and were now devouring the crabs they had caught and cooked.

"Mama will be waiting to see what we got for supper," Mahalia said, looking up at her big brother. "You eat it all up?"

"No," said Peter with a smile. He was six years older than she. "Look what I got for Mama!"

Mahalia peeked into the burlap bag and saw a baby alligator, along with crabs and shrimps. She smiled. One of her favorite dishes was alligator tail baked with onions and herbs. Since her five brothers and sisters liked the same foods she did, they often scrambled for the food at the Jackson table until Mama or Papa stopped the fighting and doled out equal portions to everyone.

The thunder clamored and the two children hurried home. Mahalia thought how much the thunder sounded like the big drum in the marching band.

"What you brought home this time?" asked Charity Jackson, their mother. When Charity spilled the contents of the bag on the table, she smiled. She poked the fire in the iron stove that warmed the family in winter and cooked the family's food all year around. Mahalia noticed that Mama had plenty of driftwood

from the river and coal from the railroad tracks. She
was glad Mama had enough, because it was one of
her jobs to hunt for fuel and she didn't like going out
in the rain to find it.

The children got ready for bed early that night.
Tomorrow everyone would have to get up early for
church. The Mount Moriah Baptist Church was not
far from the Jackson house and almost every Sunday
the whole family walked the short distance together.
One reason Mahalia looked forward to going to church
was that her father preached there every Sunday. Her
father, John Andrew Jackson, preached good sermons
from the Good Book and led the people in singing.
She was proud of her papa who, on week days, worked
as a stevedore, helping load and unload boats at the
dock. On Saturdays he was a barber. Sundays he did
himself proud standing before the congregation
preaching God's Word.

As Mahalia lay in bed, this Saturday night, she
listened to the patter, patter, patter of the raindrops
on the roof and the splashing of the water dripping
into the buckets and pans Mama had placed under
the holes in the roof. Finally she fell asleep.

In the morning Mama braided Mahalia's hair
tightly and laid out a clean dress for her to wear. The
sun was shining and the walk to church was pleasant.
Outside the church, people gathered to visit with one
another. They said, "Good morning!" as Mahalia
and her mama passed by.

Mahalia followed her mother to the front pew. Papa
was already standing up front by the pulpit. He was
a light-colored Negro whom Mahalia thought was the
handsomest, as well as the kindest, man in the world.

The people filed into the hot church. Since the windows were open, flies buzzed about.

After Papa's sermon, Mahalia was anxious to join

in the singing. Some of the songs told about where Jesus lived and walked and talked.

"Someday I'm going to the land where our Lord was," the little girl promised herself. And then she was caught up in the beat of the tambourines that the worshipers shook while they sang. The songs were so loud that sometimes Mahalia covered her ears with her hands and shivered in delight. People shouted during their singing. Their bodies swayed with the rhythm; they stamped their feet and clapped their hands.

Little Mahalia clapped her hands, too. When people cried out for God's love, she stamped her feet. Since they sang the simply worded songs over and over, Mahaliah memorized them without effort.

The tom-tom beat of the spirituals was a contagious rhythm to Mahalia. She remembered that her father had told her, "These are spirituals. They came from the need to bolster spirits in the long, dark days of slavery." She didn't know exactly what they meant, but she did know the songs were old and that they came from people like her grandfather who had been slaves on the Gumpstump cotton plantation deep in Louisiana's backwoods.

She had no way of knowing that the music she heard and loved was, in part, African spiritual tradition. In early African culture, "praise songs" were sung after any event, such as a child's tooth falling out, the coming of visitors, the desire for a person's safe return, and so on.

Mahalia Sang

When Mahalia was almost five years old, she decided she was ready to try out for the choir. One Wednesday, when she knew the choir was having tryouts, she dressed herself as if for Sunday services. She rubbed vaseline on her legs so they would shine clean and pretty. Then, pushing a chair to the wall where her Sunday dress hung on a high hook, she reached for the dress and put it on.

Mahalia walked slowly toward the church. Water Street was dusty since there had been no rain for several days. Mahalia felt quivery inside because she knew she would have to stand up and sing all by herself. But she wasn't worried about not knowing the songs—she knew them all.

When Mahalia came to the church she smoothed her dress with her hands, pulled open the heavy church door, and walked in. She felt alone and afraid as she slipped along the mourner's bench and waited for her turn to try out.

"Next!" the choir master called.

The little girl stepped forward and began to sing in a soft low voice, "I'm glad, I'm glad." As the song went on, she let her feelings go. She forgot about the people who were watching and listening. As she sang, her voice grew in volume.

When Mahalia finished singing, there was silence in the church. People stared at her. Some people who had been passing by had come into the church during her song.

Mahalia's heart pounded. What did the stares and the silence mean?

Then the choir master's voice called out, "Tell the little girl with the big voice she is now a member of the Mount Moriah's Choir."

"Thank You, Lord," whispered Mahalia.

Mahalia thought that being in the choir would be all she'd ever want. But as the days went by, she had another want. She wanted her mother to be well again. She tried to be cheerful so Mama wouldn't know how fearful she was.

One day she skipped into the house humming the Mardi Gras song, "If I Ever Cease to Love."

"Mahalia!" her mama called out weakly. "Come here, child."

"Mama, I brought you these pretty flowers to make you feel better," Mahalia, said, thrusting out a bouquet of wild flowers.

Her mother took the flowers without appearing even to notice them. She was agitated about something. "I don't never want to hear you singing that Mardi Gras song again," her mama said in a hoarse voice. Then she swallowed as if it were difficult for her to speak. "Mardi Gras music and church music ain't the same thing."

"Why's that, Mama? They both sound good to me. I like them both."

"You got to choose between 'em," her mother went on. "It's like choosing between God and the devil."

"How's that, Mama?" asked Mahalia.

"You can't have it both ways," her mother explained. "Mardi Gras music is sinnin' music. Church music is praisin' the Lord music."

Mahalia was puzzled, but she said, "I'll remember that, Mama."

She stroked her mother's feverish forehead. No one, not even the doctor, seemed to know what sickness Mama had. Mahalia could see her mother grow weaker and weaker every day.

The next morning Mahalia took Mama some tea to sip. "Mahalia," her mama said in a voice as gentle as the early morning chirp of a wren. "I worry about you. If anything happens to me, don't let Papa's cousins take you. Hear?''

"Oh, Mama! Don't talk like that!" Mahalia blinked to keep back the tears.

Her mother laid her finger tips against Mahalia's mouth to quiet her. Talking was hard for Mama, but she went on, "Papa's cousins are part of Ma Rainey's Minstrels. Ma's a blues singer who tours around the South. I don't want you to be no blues singer."

"No, Mama." Mahalia's voice quavered.

One day Mahalia brought her mother an especially pretty bouquet. It was made up of many different flowers which grew along the levee. She skipped into the house and called out, "Mama!"

But the stillness in the house made her feel like whispering. Something was wrong, terribly wrong. Then she saw that her mother's bed was empty.

"Mama! Mama!" she whispered as tears spilled down her cheeks.

Mahalia wanted to run and run and run. As she started out the door, her father came into the room. She ran to him and buried her face in his shoulder.

She felt Papa's arms holding her close. He murmured, "My little chocolate drop. My dear little chocolate drop. Your Mama's safe now. She ain't sufferin' no more."

Mahalia cried, and Papa cried with her.

"Better dry your tears," he said finally. "Some neighbors is comin' with the vittles."

Mahalia looked toward the door and saw neighbor women bringing in kettles of cooked pigs' feet, baked alligator tail, black-eyed beans and rice, corn bread, and chitterlings.

Some people patted Mahalia on the head and said, "Sorry." Some people looked at her and broke into tears. Other people shook their heads, clucked their tongues, and strode away.

Women from the Holiness Church who belonged
to the burial society held the money to pay the under-
taker. They seemd to be disagreeing over which
church Charity's funeral should be held in, the
Holiness Church, or Saint John's Church out at the
Gumpstump Plantation. Their voices sent out scratchy
noises into the room. Mahalia wished they would stop
arguing.

When the ladies began talking even faster and
louder, Aunt Duke came to the doorway. All talking
stopped.

Mahalia liked Aunt Duke, a strong-looking woman
with dark brown skin and gray eyes. She carried
herself like the leader of the band.

"Charity asked me to see to it that she was buried
in the graveyard at the plantation after services at the
old Saint John's Baptist Church," Aunt Duke told
them. Her manner was firm.

The ladies remained quiet. Mahalia was glad Aunt
Duke knew what her mother wanted.

"First she will have her funeral at Mount Moriah
Baptist Church were her husband is the pastor, and
then her final burial will be from Saint John's," Aunt
Duke said with such positiveness that no one cared
to argue about it.

Mahalia tried not to sleep the night of the wake.
The wake was to last all night she was told. Members
of the church, neighbors, and relatives talked and
prayed and sang through the night. But Mahalia could
not keep her eyelids from closing when it came to an
hour past her bedtime.

The next morning Aunt Duke woke her. "It's
time," was all she said as she reached for Mahalia's
Sunday dress and helped her put it on.

At the funeral Mahalia listened to the sermons.
There were several preachers. They talked about Jesus

out in the wilderness; they talked about Jesus in the Garden of Gethsemane.

"Some day I'll go to the land of Jesus and see some of those places," thought Mahalia.

Then she followed Aunt Duke to the train station where the family boarded a train.

A wagon met the train and carried them to the river. Mahalia saw them put her mother's casket on a little white skiff. Aunt Duke took Mahalia's hand as they got on another boat. Rowers rowed the family across to where country people, who had known Charity as a child, were waiting to bury her in a little cemetery next to the church. Mahalia watched and wondered. She would always remember that scene as long as she lived.

Mahalia cried that day until, because of her faith in God, she began accepting her sorrow. "Mama's with God," she told herself.

When all the relatives were again assembled in the Jackson home, they talked about who was going to take care of Mahalia, age five, and William, age ten. The other children had already been divided between five of Mahalia's aunts.

Aunt Duke cleared her throat and eveyone fell silent. They all admired Aunt Duke because she was a high-class cook for a wealthy white family over on St. George Avenue where the society folk lived. She was such a good cook that she got ten dollars a week, which everyone knew was high pay for Negro help.

Aunt Duke spoke up, "I'll take them both," she said.

The room was quiet. Papa sat with his head in his hands. "Raisin' up young ones is woman's work," he murmured. "Besides, I work so many hours, I'd never be with 'em."

Mahalia was remembering that Mama didn't want

the children to go with Papa's cousins. Mama would be pleased that Aunt Duke would take her and William.

Aunt Duke was not much for showing affection, but her husband was just the opposite, warm and affectionate. Aunt Duke was a church-going woman. Mama once told her them's the best kind there is.

"Thank You, Lord, for the home William and me is going to have," Mahalia prayed.

That night Mahalia and her brother went to live with Aunt Duke and Uncle Emanuel Paul.

Life with Aunt Duke

Mahalia cried more tears that night after she went to her new bed at Aunt Duke's house. She couldn't imagine what it would be like not to have her brothers and sisters in the house. At least she would have William.

As she lay in the darkness, sounds from the outside insisted on being heard. There were the toots of the river boats and the shrill cries from the trains. A loud phonograph played a record about an insect that destroyed cotton. "De Boll Weevil is a little black bug. . ."

The blues singer sounded like Ma Rainey. Everyone on Water Street talked about Ma Rainey's great contralto voice. Mahalia shaped her lips the way she thought Ma Rainey shaped hers to get notes to come out loud and clear.

Then she felt guilty. Church people didn't sing the blues. Still, she liked to listen to Ma Rainey.

The next morning Mahalia had her first cooking lesson.

"Always save the fat," Aunt Duke said as she showed Mahalia how to fry bacon. "I uses the fat to season collard and mustard greens. Gotta have fat for cornbread and such, too."

The family sat down to a breakfast of bacon, eggs, cornbread, and syrup.

Uncle Emanuel took William with him as a yard boy for a white family, while Aunt Duke nodded to Mahalia to follow her to the garden patch beside the house.

"This is how to weed the garden," Aunt Duke said, giving Mahalia a hoe.

For hours, Mahalia hoed the rows of okra, green beans, red beans, tomatoes, pumpkin and corn.

A robin perched himself on a limb of a nearby magnolia tree and trilled a song.

"That's mighty pretty singin' " Mahalia called to him. "Singin' always makes work easier."

When the sun was hot in the sky, Aunt Duke said, "You gotta know how to work with your hands. All black people do. That's the way things is."

"Yes 'um," replied Mahalia.

"Now I is gonna make some soap from them drippin's on the back of the stove," Aunt Duke said.

Making soap was a hot and tedious job. But as they worked, Aunt Duke and Mahalia sang and hummed songs they both knew and loved—"Before I'd Be a Slave I'd Be Buried in My Grave," "Children, We Shall Be Free," "Walk Together, Children, Don't Get Weary."

That evening Mahalia washed herself in the big tin tub in the kitchen, put on the clean dress Aunt Duke gave her, and together she and Aunt Duke walked to church for prayer services.

"We'll go to prayer services every week-day night," Aunt Duke told her.

"Yes 'um," said Mahalia, nodding.

As the two of them strode toward the church, Mahalia listened to phonographs playing in many of the homes they passed. "That's Bessie Smith singin' the 'St. Louis Blues'," Aunt Duke told Mahalia as they went by a shack where the porch sagged to the ground. "That's the devil's music," she concluded with a shake of her head.

"Yes 'um," said Mahalia, feeling wicked because she liked to listen to Bessie Smith sing.

But Mahalia didn't have time to think of wickedness as the days went by. She was too busy learning new skills from Aunt Duke. She learned to make mattresses of corn shucks and soft, gray Spanish moss that hung from the trees.

"You tuck the shucks and the moss into these mattress covers I been makin' from cement sacks," Aunt Duke told her one morning before she went to work. "You get 'em all done afore I come home. Hear?"

"Yes 'um," said Mahalia.

The next day Aunt Duke told Mahalia, "Scrub the floor of this here house. Use da red brick and lye, and that cypress wood will get a pretty pale color."

"Yes 'um," said Mahalia.

When Mahalia was seven, having finished the first grade, she was ready for her first job.

It was Aunt Belle, her mother's youngest sister (who was twelve years old), who got Mahalia her first job.

"You come with me," Aunt Belle told Mahalia. Mahalia thought how pretty her aunt was with her full mouth of white teeth and her straight wide-nostriled nose.

Mahalia followed her Aunt Belle to the home of the Ryder family. There were five Ryder children.

Mahalia tiptoed into the immaculate kitchen which was all shiny white, with seven high-backed chairs spaced evenly about a round oak table.

"We'll start breakfast and then we have to help the childrens get ready for school, put away their nightgowns, serve them their breakfast, and wash the dishes," Aunt Belle explained.

"Then can we go to school?" asked Mahalia.

"Yes," said Aunt Belle. "We'll have to run like the devil's chasin' us to get there on time."

Mahalia followed Aunt Belle through the chores and soon learned what to do.

"You're smart," Aunt Belle told her. "You learn quick."

The sounds in the house were happy sounds of talk and laughter and fun. Mahalia liked the Ryders.

Mahalia also liked the left-over food the Ryders gave her and Aunt Belle to take home. She liked the children's old clothing Mrs. Ryder bundled up for her to wear. But most of all she was glad for the two dollars a week in cash that she could take home to Aunt Duke. Money was scarce and Mahalia knew that she and William were eating their Aunt and Uncle out of any spare money they might have.

On Saturdays Mahalia didn't have to work at the Ryders. This was the day she often visited her papa at the barber shop. She liked the walk to the barber shop because she could listen to music all the way. Sometimes she saw little black boys clicking hollow-dried bones against each other in a rhythmic beat. Sometimes she saw men sitting together at street corners making music by blowing into empty glass gallon jugs. Often she fell into step with other children behind the Eureka Brass Band as they led a funeral march into the cemetery playing, "When the Saints Go Marching In."

One Saturday Aunt Duke said, "Tell your father that you need shoes. It ain't right for you to go to school barefoot."

Mahalia jumped from her place at the table and ran out into the street. She was always happy when she had permission to go see Papa.

Soon she was marching with the Eureka Brass Band humming, ''When the Saints Go Marching In,'' and trying to sing parts of the song the way she thought Bessie Smith would.

She turned the corner, leaving the Band, and made her way toward the barber shop. When she got to the shop she slid into a chair. Her father didn't see her at first. He was intent on trimming a customer's beard. Mahalia sat quietly. She wished she could see him more often, but Papa's new wife made it very clear that she didn't want Papa's children around.

Finally Mr. Jackson looked up. ''How's my little chocolate drop?'' he asked with a broad grin.

''Aunt Duke says I shouldn't go to school without shoes, Papa,'' Mahalia told him. ''She says I should ask you for some money.''

Her father searched through four trouser pockets. Evidently there was no money in any of them. Mr. Jackson scratched his head and frowned.

''Here's the fifteen cents I owe you,'' said the customer.

Mr. Jackson gave the fifteen cents to Mahalia. ''Tell Aunt Duke I'll give her more when I can,'' he said.

Mahalia nodded. She clenched her fist over the coins.

''Bye,'' she said and left the shop.

As she walked sadly back home, she scarcely heard the street music, the Jew's harp players, or the street vendors.

''Lord,'' she prayed, ''you sure got your work cut out for you. You gotta help me 'cause life ain't easy.''

Life Ain't Easy

School stopped for Mahalia when she finished the eighth grade. She was a big girl for her thirteen years. Now that she was out of school she could work full time for the white folks in the fancy neighborhoods of New Orleans. Sometimes the days were twelve hours long. Mahalia was a good worker, rubbing clothes on a scrub board and ironing backbreaking hours on an ironing board. She could do a man's shirt in three minutes and a handkerchief in one.

Mahalia sang as she worked. "I'm So Glad Jesus Lifted Me Up" was one of her favorite songs. She folded the pillow slips and took down the ironing board. She was especially anxious to get home early on this day. Uncle Emanuel was coming home. He had been working in Chicago as a bricklayer, and Mahalia missed him. She was also lonesome for Fred, Aunt Duke's grown son, who had gone to Kansas City to live.

As she hurried out the back door, she heard a scream from the east side of the yard. She ran to the spot and there on the ground was Sara, one of the Ryder children. Her face was pale white and gushes of blood spurted from her right leg. Mahalia felt the pounding of fear inside of her. She did not want to show Sara how frightened she was.

"Mahalia," moaned Sara. "I fell out of the tree. My kitten was up there."

"Hush, child," Mahalia whispered soothingly. "I'll tend you." Mahalia's hands checked for broken bones.

Finding none she said, "Praise the Lord."

Then Mahalia gathered little Sara into her strong arms and carried her into the kitchen, where she laid her on the long kitchen table. Soon she had Sara's stocking ripped away and was washing the wound.

Sara watched her with tear-filled eyes. "It hurts, Mahalia."

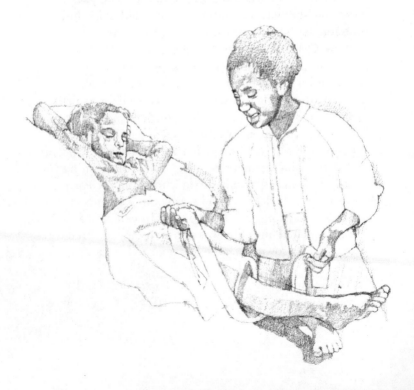

"I knows that, child," Mahalia answered sooth-ingly. "I'll be as gentle as I can. I'm goin' to disinfect the wound with this medicine, and then I'm goin' to bandage it all up nice, and then I'm callin' the doctor."

"Will it hurt?" asked Sara.

"Yes," replied Mahalia. She dressed the wound. Sara whimpered.

"You are a brave child," Mahalia told Sara as she crossed the kitchen to the telephone.

While Mahalia and Sara waited for the doctor, Mahalia carried Sara to the cane-seated rocker and began singing, "Standing in the Need of Prayer." Sara's big blue eyes never left Mahalia's face. "I love you, Mahalia," Sara said.

When the doctor came, he was quick to inspect Mahalia's work.

"You'd make a fine nurse," said the doctor, nod-ding his head in approval. "You've cleansed the wound nicely and I can take over from here. We'll need a few stitches. Will you please assist me?"

"Yes, doctor," said Mahalia. She felt proud that the doctor asked her.

"Don't leave me, Mahalia," Sara pleaded.

"I'm right here, child," Mahalia replied, patting Sara's hand.

Finally, Mahalia left the Ryder house. The twilight was gathering. Sounds of the city pleased Mahalia as she made her way home. The sounds had a familiar rhythm. When she got home, Aunt Duke was busy at the stove and the kitchen was filled with the good smells of cooking food.

Uncle Emanuel jumped out of his chair and hugged Mahalia.

"It is good to have you home, Uncle," Mahalia said. "We want to hear all about Chicago."

"Serve up some of this food," commanded Aunt Duke. "Talkin' is for later."

Mahalia's eyes scanned the table to make sure everything was perfect and then she asked, "Kin I say the blessing tonight? I feel so grateful for Sara and Uncle Emanuel and oh, just everything."

"Bless this house, O Lord, and we thank Thee for this food," prayed Mahalia.

The food was good. As usual there was plenty of it. Mahalia heaped her plate twice.

"Tell us about Chicago," Mahalia said, smiling broadly at her uncle.

"It's different up there in Illinois," Uncle Emanuel said.

"How do you mean 'different'?" asked Mahalia.

"Well," Uncle Emanuel began speaking thoughtfully. "Black people eat at white restaurants, ride taxi cabs with white drivers, buy clothes where the white people buy their clothes, and blacks can choose their trades more."

Mahalia sat stunned. She thought, "If the good Lord is willin', I'll save my money. I'll work hard. And then I'll go up north to Chicago where I won't have to clean white people's houses nor wash their dirty clothes. I'll be a nurse!"

These were her thoughts the rest of the week. Even on Sunday morning, Baptismal Sunday, Mahalia's thoughts were of Chicago. On this very special Sunday the family arrived early and took their places on one of the wooden benches near the front of the church.

The little church soon filled, and John Jackson walked in and mounted the pulpit. Mahalia was proud of her father as he led the prayers and gave a strong sermon on loving the Lord with all your heart and with all your soul.

"My daddy's a good preacher," she thought proudly.

Then her father announced that the time had come for Baptism. The women, all dressed in white, rose and led the way out of the church, singing, "Let's Go Down to the River Jordan." They marched down the street to another street that led them to the Mississippi River. Mahalia's voice soared, loud and clear.

At the river she listened to her father leading prayers. She watched him baptize people who professed faith in Jesus as their Lord and Savior. Mahalia remembered the day when she was lowered into the waters of baptism. That had been a perfect day.

Mahalia thought this was a perfect day, too. But that night she was wakened by the sounds of crying. It was Aunt Duke, who was holding a telegram. "What is the matter?" asked Mahalia.

"Fred is dead," answered Aunt Duke.

Mahalia drew in her breath. Her cousin Fred was her favorite cousin. She knew how much Aunt Duke loved this great big, jet-black man with pearly teeth. Fred worked hard around the docks. He loved music and he bought all the blues and jazz records he could. Mahalia loved his records. Even though Aunt Duke forbid Mahalia to listen to them, Mahalia enjoyed listening to them when she could.

The next few days were full of shock. Mahalia's mind was troubled. She had been too young to feel the full impact of her mother's death, but she was feeling the finality of death when her cousin died. They brought Fred back to be buried at the little church where Mahalia worshiped. A wake went on all night and lodge bands formed outside the church and played for hours.

The Chicago Dream

As Mahalia dreamed of going up North to become a nurse, she noticed many people began drifting away from New Orleans. Some young black men began to go from their jobs on the river to jobs on the trains. They became chefs and waiters and Pullman car porters.

Her Uncle Porter was one of the men she knew who had advanced this way. After he was headwaiter in a big boarding house in New Orleans, he decided to move up to the railroads.

In those days (about 1927) the trains were in their height of popularity. Steamboats were on the way out. The trains which had sleeping cars and elegant dining cars, streamed out of New Orleans constantly.

"I used to take care of four hundred people a day in that dining car," bragged Uncle Porter. "I was the fastest second cook on the line."

Young black men Mahalia knew took pride in their food service. They wore starched white jackets and they polished the brass floors in those railroad car kitchens. And they learned about the country they traveled through.

Mahalia sighed. If only she could get away and amount to something, too!

On her fifteenth birthday she went down to the barber shop to see her father.

"I want to go North and have a chance to help people by being a nurse," she told her father.

He smiled his kindly smile, put his hands on her shoulders, and looked straight into her eyes. "Before you make such a big move, let me go to Chicago and see what it's like," he said. "I got me some money saved. I've been thinkin' of leavin' in about a week."

"If it's all they say it is, will you stay?" Mahalia asked. There was joy and hope in her voice.

"Maybe," Mr. Jackson replied.

Weeks went by. Mahalia had no word from her father.

"Your father is back," Aunt Duke told her one day. "I saw him by the water front. He wants to talk to you."

Mahalia fled the house and ran to her father's barber shop.

"Papa," she called out, "tell me. Tell me about Chicago!"

Mr. Jackson took the barber's cape off a client, pocketed the money the man gave him, and turned toward Mahalia.

"I didn't like Chicago," he said. "That's why I didn't write or nuthin'. I thought I'd get to like it, then I'd send you word."

"Why didn't you like Chicago, Papa?" Mahalia asked. She was so disappointed that tears were pushing against her eyelids.

"I got scared," her father said. "I kept hearin'

about Al Capone and all them gangsters, and I figured I'd get killed by them sooner or later. Besides, that city's too big for a body to get used to.''

When Mahalia left her father, she felt depressed. What he told her was not what she wanted to hear.

''I'm going to go north anyway,'' she murmured aloud. ''My church will protect me from gangsters.''

Mahalia held on to her dream; the dream of going north and becoming a nurse.

It was when Mahalia was sixteen that the dream began to materialize. Aunt Hannah, who lived in Chicago, was in New Orleans for a visit. She wanted Mahalia to go back to Chicago with her.

''She ain't goin','' Aunt Duke said.

''There's a chance for a girl in Chicago,'' Aunt Hannah argued.

''It's a wicked city and I ain't throwin' Mahalia into nuthin' like that,'' Aunt Duke argued back.

Aunt Duke turned toward Mahalia and laid her hands on Mahalia's forearms.

''You want to be a nurse,'' Aunt Hannah said. ''Aunt Duke told me that herself. How can you learn to be a nurse here where there isn't even a hospital for black people to go to when they're sick? So there's no place for a girl to go to get any nurse's training if she's black.''

Mahalia hesitated a moment, casting a look at the disapproving Aunt Duke.

''It's cold in Chicago'' Mahalia said in a low voice.

''It *is* cold there in winter,'' Aunt Hannah agreed. ''The city is noisy. A person has to work hard just to make a living. But you have a chance to make something of yourself.''

''I depend on her to write letters for me and help me visit the sick in our church,'' Aunt Duke said firmly.

"She's not the only girl in New Orleans whose gone through the eighth grade," Hannah snapped back with a quick answer to Aunt Duke's protests.

When it was time for church, Mahalia walked behind Aunt Duke and Uncle Emanuel, with Aunt Hannah beside her. At the church she left them and sat with the choir behind the preacher. In her sadness, she didn't know what to do. She hoped they would sing a song that would carry her troubles away. Looking out over the congregation, she saw people she had known all her life. They were mostly servants who had been working for white people from the time they started grammar school. They'd have no choice but being some white folks' servant till they became bent over, worked-out old men and women. She had to have a chance to become more than that!

Mahalia bowed her head and prayed. "Dear Lord, I want a chance. I want to go north and study to be a good nurse. Please help Aunt Duke understand."

God's presence was building in a song. Mahalia felt the strength of it in her throat. She threw back her head and raised her hands with the palms outstretched. Mahalia heard her deep-throated notes circle the church.

> Sometimes I feel like a motherless chile,
> Sometimes I feel like a motherless chile,
> Far, far away from home, a long ways from home,
> Then I get down on my knees an' pray,
> Get down on my knees an' pray.

The church rocked with Mahalia. The song took wings over Water Street. People passing by stopped and began to sing. Inside the Mount Moriah Church, people swung with the music. They moved from side to side in rhythm. People clapped their hands and patted their feet. Mahalia sank to her knees. Some people in the congregation wept.

"Thank You, Jesus. Thank You, Jesus!" was heard all over the church as people tried to show their appreciation for Mahalia's singing. Her singing had lightened their hearts as she sang of the way to accept Jesus as the Lord and Savior.

Mahalia remained on her knees as if being there in this subservient position would bring her the answer to whether or not she should defy Aunt Duke, use the money she had saved from her years of working for white folks, and take off for the Windy City with Aunt Hannah.

After church Mahalia and Aunt Hannah walked out with the congregation.

"You sing real good," one woman said.

"You got the gift of singing, Mahalia!" said another.

Mahalia was warmed by all the praise. She began to wonder if she should give up all these good friends, her church, listening to her father's preaching, and Aunt Duke.

When they got back to Aunt Duke's, Mahalia's nostrils extended with pleasure. She could smell the collard greens and salt pork that Aunt Duke had put on the back of the old cook stove before leaving for church.

Mahalia raised her head high. She was ready to tell Aunt Duke she had made up her mind. At dinner Mahalia made her announcement.

"I'm going to Chicago," she said firmly.

"You just forget about going to Chicago," Aunt Duke said. "You stay here where I can watch over you."

"I'm a big girl now," Mahalia argued, rising to her feet. She was taller than Aunt Duke, and with her hair piled high on her head she looked older than her sixteen years.

"It is so wicked up there in the North," Aunt Duke

said, pointing a finger at Mahalia, "that you might even stop goin' to church!"

"Oh, Aunt Duke!" Mahalia cried, "I would never, never stop going to church. Never!"

Aunt Duke's eyes grew misty. "I'm sure goin' to miss you a heap," she said softly.

Chicago

On a December morning Mahalia went to the railroad station to catch the train for Chicago. It would be a long trip to Chicago, two nights and a day.

Mahalia smiled when she saw the crowd of friends and relatives at the station to bid her goodbye. These dear people! Did she really want to leave everything she loved for the uncertainty that awaited her up North?

She and Aunt Hannah took their places at the end of the Jim Crow ticket window. Aunt Duke was hanging on her arm as if she were parting with her forever. The ticket agent took care of the white passengers first. Then he came over to the window where the blacks were waiting.

Aunt Hannah muttered under her breath about how dare he treat people this way!

Mahalia sighed. Aunt Hannah had forgotten that black people had learned to keep quiet in New Orleans.

"How are you feelin'?" Aunt Duke asked, looking up into Mahalia's face.

"I feel poorly," Mahalia answered just as the ticket agent opened the Jim Crow window.

He was a blond man. Mahalia judged he was in his twenties. His manner was arrogant and he talked to each ticket buyer any way he pleased.

Mahalia slipped Aunt Hannah the money for her ticket when they finally were next at the window. "Can't you hurry?" Aunt Hannah said. "We've got to walk the whole length of this here platform to get to the Jim Crow train."

"Now see here, nigger woman," the ticket agent snarled at her, "you keep a civil tongue in your head or maybe I won't even sell you a ticket!"

Mahalia nudged Aunt Duke to be quiet.

"And where do you think you're going?" the agent asked.

"Chicago," Aunt Hannah answered.

"Nigger-loving Chicago, huh? I wish they'd take all of you."

Mahalia nudged Aunt Duke again.

Aunt Hannah handed Mahalia the two one-way tickets, picked up some of the luggage, leaving the heavier pieces and the lunchbasket for Mahalia to carry, and hurried to the last coach.

Mahalia looked at the interior of the coach and clucked her tongue in disgust. It was exactly as she had been told it would be. Many blacks in New Orleans called this coach the Chickenbone Express because there were always bones littering the floor, thrown there by previous passengers.

"If I had a scrub bucket full of suds I could do this train a lot of good," Mahalia told Aunt Hannah.

Just as the two women got seated, the train whistle let out its warning that the train was ready to move. A big bell clanged. The train gave several jerks then it began to move forward. She was on her way to Chicago!

Mahalia rested her head on the back of the seat and mentally recited the advertisement she had memorized. The advertisement was one she had clipped from the *Chicago Defender*.

Provident Hospital and Training School for Nurses offers young colored women a three-year course in the practice and theory of nursing. Graduates eligible for registration from any state. Classes now forming. For information apply to Superintendent, Provident Hospital, 16 West 36 Street, Chicago, Illinois.

Would she be accepted? She had nursed children and grown-ups all the years she had worked in white peoples' homes. They said she had a gentle touch and was a consolation to have around when people were

sick, but was that and an eighth grade education
enough to make her eligible at the nurses' school?

Aunt Hannah's voice cut into her thoughts. "You
have to get a coat up in Chicago. When that breeze
comes off the lake in December, *whoeee*, it's mighty
cold."

I'll have to earn some money first," Mahalia said.

Mahalia pulled the sweater closer around her. Some
day when she was a nurse she'd have a proper coat
to keep her warm.

The train jostled along. Its movement loosed the
lid on the basket of food from Aunt Duke. The aroma
of chicken was strong in Mahalia's nostrils. " 'Spose
we ought to eat?" she asked Aunt Hannah. The comfort of food helped Mahalia tolerate her troubles.

She forgot her fears when she saw all the fried
chicken and biscuits and yams in the basket. Mahalia
said a table grace and she and Aunt Hannah ate their
fill, glancing out the window occasionally to watch the
steady flow of the Mississippi River. The tracks ran
parallel to the river for miles.

It was getting dark. Mahalia put the basket in neat
order and closed her eyes. She heard the people in
the train speaking in low voices. A baby cried a
complaint.

Mahalia was too cold to sleep. The fire from the
locomotive lit up the landscape, but didn't warm the
passengers. Mahalia saw a row of shanties with their
gardens of greens, their lean-to chicken coops, and
their single pigs rooting around in their pens. Mahalia
sighed. Miles and miles of shanties just like in New
Orleans.

When morning finally came, Mahalia and Aunt
Hannah ate their breakfast from what was left in the
basket. It was a long trip to Chicago—two nights and

a day. Then the train slowed down. It came to a net-
work of railroad tracks with more trains than Mahalia
could count. Beyond the tracks Mahalia could see tall
buildings. They were taller than she had imagined.

Aunt Hannah and Mahalia got the luggage down
from the racks above their heads. They climbed down
from the train and walked into the depot.

"We'll get a cup of coffee," Aunt Hannah said,
leading the way to the coffee shop. Mahalia didn't
see any black people at the counter. She wondered
if they would be served. A black person couldn't go
into a coffee shop and be served. Was Aunt Hannah
sure they could get a cup of coffee?

Aunt Hannah motioned her to sit beside her at the
counter. Aunt Hannah then called out, "Two cups
of coffee, please!"

Mahalia squirmed.

"Coming right up!" the waitress called back, fill-
ing two cups with the hot brew.

Mahalia stared at the waitress. She had never been
served by a white person before.

"We'll have to get a cab," Aunt Hannah said, as
they left the depot.

The wind was blowing snow around and it was so
cold that Mahalia felt even her bones shaking. She
started walking down the street but Aunt Hannah
called her back.

She had waved to a cab driven by a white man.
Mahalia knew it was against the law in New Orleans
to ride in a cab driven by a white person. But while
these thoughts were going around in her mind, the
cabbie put their luggage in the trunk of the cab, asked
the address, and stepped on the gas.

He drove them to the proper address on the South
Side of the city where another aunt, Aunt Alice, was

living with her children. It was at the corner of Thirtieth and Prairie Avenue in a big brick building. The place had an iron gate and rugs on the stairs that made the place look fancy to Mahalia. She could hardly believe that black people lived in such an elegant place.

Mahalia took a deep breath. "What's that smell?" she asked.

"The Chicago stockyards is near here," Aunt Hannah explained.

In the apartment, Hannah showed Mahalia the rooms Aunt Alice had. They saw the small living room in which there was the couch Aunt Hannah slept on. Then they went past a room rented to a railroad dining-car waiter. When they came to the dining room, Mahalia was told that here was where Alice's son, Nathaniel, had a bed. Then Mahalia was taken to a drafty sunporch. This was where she would sleep.

It wasn't long before Aunt Alice came home.

"Hello, Mahalia," Aunt Alice greeted her. There was no real joy in the greeting.

"What's wrong?" Mahalia asked.

"I've lost my job," Aunt Alice explained. "But I got some names of people who need laundry done."

"Don't your lodger pay good?" Mahalia asked.

"Sure. He pays enough for the gas and electricity, but we need fifty dollars a month for the rent," Aunt Alice explained.

"I want to do my share," Mahalia said.

"Here's the name of a person who needs laundry done," said Aunt Alice, giving Mahalia a slip of paper with a name and address written on it.

"Laundry?" Mahalia asked under her breath. What about nursing and making something of her life? Wasn't that why she left New Orleans?

Wash Tubs and
Choir Practice

It was dark and cold the next morning when
Mahalia and Aunt Alice left for work. Aunt Alice
climbed the stairs to the elevated train with Mahalia.
She had to take another train, so she gave Mahalia
explicit instructions.

Aunt Alice waited until Mahalia's train came and
then she waved goodbye. The first thing Mahalia
noticed was that she was the only black in the whole
train. Nobody else seemed to notice that or her. People
sat gazing out into the lightening day or were
absorbed in their newspapers.

Mahalia shivered. She watched the snow blow and
swirl in the street lights and the sun just starting to
come up. She felt lonely and afraid. The cold and the
noise seemed to beat on her.

When the train stopped at the station Aunt Alice
had named, Mahalia got out and waited for the
crosstown train. When it came, she took a seat near

the door and counted five stops, as Aunt Alice had
told her to do. She got off and went down to the street.
She found Herndon Avenue and walked to the house
with the number written on her slip of paper.

A woman in a bathrobe let her in. She pointed to
the door in the kitchen that led down to the basement.
Mahalia nodded and went down to the cold, dingy
laundry where soiled clothing and bedding was piled
high on a rickety table.

Mahalia filled the tubs and began her work. She
was cold and hungry and discouraged. She needed
to feel close to the Lord. She began to sing, "His eye
is on the sparrow, and I know He watches me. I
sing—"

"Please sing more!" a young voice pleaded.

Mahalia looked up. A small girl was sitting on the
steps watching her.

"Wah's your name?" the girl asked.

"Mahalia Jackson."

"You sing real good, Mahalia Jackson. Please sing more."

Mahalia sang. It lightened the heavy work to sing about what was in her heart, to sing for the Lord.

Mahalia worked for other people in the days to come. She earned a dollar a day and carfare. She was becoming accustomed to the city, especially the South Side.

In 1928 the South Side was the second largest Negro city in the world, second only to New York's Harlem. It started on Eighteenth Street and ran as far south as Fifty-fifth Street. It was squeezed in between the stockyards to the west and the white neighborhoods along the shores of Lake Michigan to the east. It was seven miles long and two miles wide. It held about three hundred thousand Negroes.

One day Mahalia came home from a job of twelve hours of ironing. Aunt Alice met her at the door. She was crying.

"Hannah's had a heart attack," she said. "I called the doctor and he gave Hannah some pills. He don't know for sure that she will live."

Mahalia let the tears roll down her cheeks. She hurried to her room and dropped to her knees. She prayed fervently for Hannah's recovery.

"That leaves only Aunt Alice to support the family," she said aloud. "I just have to pitch in and help."

With Aunt Hannah's slow recovery came the need to be quiet around the house. The children needed somewhere to go in the evenings. Aunt Alice took them with her to her church, the Greater Salem Baptist Church.

In a few weeks Mahalia met the Reverend Johnson, who had founded the church, and all his family. There

were three brothers and a sister, all around Mahalia's
age. They spent most of their spare time in church
work.

"What do you like to do most?" the sister asked.

"Sing," was Mahalia's immediate reply.

"Would you like to try out for our choir?" the
young woman asked. "Tryouts are tomorrow night."

Mahalia hurried home from her laundry job, ate
a quick supper, and was at the church before any of
the Johnsons were there.

"Please just sing along with the choir," one of the
Johnson brothers told her.

There were fifty people in the choir. They sang from
song books. Mahalia watched while the choir master
put them through their practice.

Mahalia couldn't read music from a song book. She
didn't know about the harmony or structure of chords
that the choir master talked about. She had learned
to sing by listening to the spirituals she heard in
church, to street vendors, to the records of Ma Rainey
and Bessie Smith.

She had never sung with a pianist. They did not
have pianos in the churches she went to in New
Orleans. She knew her sense of hearing was a
marvelously accurate instrument. She knew that
whatever she had learned by ear came out with deep
feeling because of her reverence for God.

"Miss Jackson," the choir master called out.

Mahalia felt numb. She could hardly make a move.

"Here goes nuthin'!" she whispered under her
breath. She stood beside the piano. The choir master
gave her some music. "Han' Me Down Yo' Silvah
Trumpet, Gabriel" was the title of the song he gave
her.

The piano sounded far away. Mahalia sang the first
words very quietly so that she could get the range.

By the time she finished the first verse, the choir room was filled with people who had come from all over the church when they heard her sing.

She became a member of the choir, and the Greater Salem Baptist Church grew to seem like her second home. She was friendly with the Johnsons, and often came back from her wash jobs on the North Side, got off the elevated train at the station nearest the church, and visited awhile with them.

Mahalia busied herself with church socials and picnics and excursions on Lake Michigan. Church services were held during the week as well as on Sunday.

She faithfully wrote Aunt Duke every week. Once she was over the ache of homesickness, she was happier in Chicago than she thought she would ever be. She held high her hope that she'd soon be studying to be a nurse and that she would be out of the washtubs and ironing boards forever.

A big part of her happiness came from singing in a quintet with four other young people, the minister's three sons (Prince, Robert, and Wilbur Johnson) and another girl, Louise Barry.

Prince Johnson worked out all the arrangements on the piano. He had his own style of playing. With Prince at the piano, the group had a "bounce" that made them popular from the start. This was the first Negro gospel group in the city.

Mahalia enjoyed the quintet. At first they sang for their own church, then invitations came from other churches.

At this time (1929) churches were struggling to keep their doors open. All during the boom days of the twenties, black people had been buying white people's churches and synagogues. There were big mortgages to pay off. The Depression had stopped the stream of money and the congregations could not meet their

mortage payments or pay for the coal to heat their churches or the electricity to light them.

Church people tried to raise a little money with special suppers and socials. The Johnson Singers helped churches raise money. The churches collected a little admission money to help toward their expenses and gave the Johnson singers as much as a $1.50 a night to show their appreciation.

The Johnson Singers sang all over the South Side. Then they began to get invitations outside the city to black churches in downstate Illinois and Indiana. They sang at the Baptist Conventions in St. Louis and Cleveland.

It was surprising to Mahalia that here she was, twenty years old, in the middle of the Great Depression, able to help Aunt Hannah and Aunt Alice, and still have several dollars in her purse for herself.

Mahalia's Vocal Lesson

People were always telling Mahalia she shouldn't let her voice go to waste. "You should take singing lessons," they told her.

"There's that great Professor DuBois," Louise Barry said. "Let's take lessons from him!"

"Who's he?" asked Mahalia.

"He's a great Negro tenor," Louise explained.

Mahalia decided to take the advice so many people had given her, but her mind was against it. She was not totally sure that she could take instruction from such a notable concert singer. She had promised Louise Barry that she would go with her for their first lesson. A promise was a sacred trust, so she was committed to go. The lesson would cost four dollars, which was a lot of money. Mahalia counted the bills in her purse once again. Four dollars of hard-earned money. This was 1932 and money was a little easier to earn than at the start of the Depression, but four dollars was four dollars.

Mahalia scratched a peep hole on the frosted glass window of the little apartment. The frost was thick and cold. She looked out on the dimly lit Chicago street and wished she could stay inside where the radiators were pounding out heat.

"I gotta go," she said aloud. "I promised the people in that little South Side Church that I'd come and sing. A promise is a promise."

She pulled on two sweaters and a knit stocking cap, then struggled into her mohair winter coat. Outside the wind swirled. Frost formed halos around the street lights. "Anyone comes out on a night like this is crazy!" Mahalia said into the woolen scarf around her neck.

At last the dim lights of the little Baptist Church in the middle of the block twinkled faint light into the night. Mahalia with renewed energy scrambled down the basement stairs and into the Sunday school room.

"Mahalia!" the people called out. There were only fourteen people in the whole room!

"You're brave to come out on a night like this," Mahalia told them.

"We want to hear you sing. Sing to us, Mahalia!"

Mahalia walked over to the old man who sat at the piano.

"I don't read music," she said. "Can you just follow along?"

"Sure, Mahalia," the old man said. "I'll just play a note here and there. I'll follow you. Give me a signal or two."

Mahalia began to sing. Fourteen people sat enraptured through "The Lord's Prayer."

Then she sang, "Steal away, steal away, steal away to Jesus."

People cried openly and begged Mahalia to sing

more . . . more . . . more. "Han' Me Down Yo' Silvah Trumpet, Gabriel"; "His Eye is on the Sparrow"; "Sometimes I Feel Like a Motherless Chile" were sung again and again until it was past eleven o'clock.

"God bless you, Mahalia," one woman said. "You've lifted my soul!"

Then, as Mahalia worked back into her two sweaters, her stocking cap and her mohair coat a little woman in shabby attire asked, "Would it be possible for you to come home with me and sing just one of your beautiful songs for Mama? Mama ain't able to come to church no more. She's poorly, you know."

Mahalia felt a tug of pity and nodded in agreement. Back out on the street, Mahalia faced the numbing wind off Lake Michigan. She trudged beside the woman until they came to a run-down apartment house. She climbed up the rickety flight of stairs and into the sparcely furnished apartment where an old woman lay on a daybed.

"Mama!" cried the little woman. "This here is Mahalia Jackson. She sings gospel. She's come to sing for you, Mama!"

The old lady's eyes opened wide. Mahalia smiled. Slowly, softly, Mahalia's deep-throated tones circled the room. "It's me, it's me, it's me, O Lord, standing in the need of prayer."

"Thank You, Jesus," the old lady said over and over again.

After a few more songs, Mahalia asked the old woman if she would like to join her in prayer.

Mahalia sank to her knees beside the old woman and, taking the shriveled hands in hers, she prayed, "Almighty and everlasting God, source of all true life, we bless Thee, we thank Thee for Thy great goodness to us. And when the work Thou hast given us to do

is ended, receive us into Thy joy and bestow upon
us the crown of everlasting glory, which fadeth not
away; through Jesus Christ our Lord. Amen.''

Silently Mahalia added a prayer that her first music
lesson would help her be a better singer.

On the day of the lesson, Mahalia finished taking
trash out to the alley while the biting wind from Lake
Michigan made her breathe deeply. Deep breathing
is good for a singer, she thought.

''With all the deep breathing I've been doing today
I should be in fine shape for my lesson tonight,'' she
said aloud.

Early that evening the El train roared its way into
her disembarking station. She got off the train with
other black women who thought themselves lucky to
have even menial labor during these days of the Great
Depression.

Once on the pavement, Mahalia started toward
Greater Salem. Her progress was slowed when she
saw the sheriff's deputies taking furniture out of a
house.

''They couldn't pay their rent,'' a woman told her.

Mahalia paused. She wondered if it would be the
Christian thing to do to give the family her four dollars
with which to pay their rent.

If she took the music lesson, would it help her make
bigger contributions later on?

Her friend, Louise, had already made the appoint-
ment with Professor DuBois. He would charge her
whether she took the lesson or not because he had
saved time for her.

Mahalia walked to the Greater Salem Baptist
Church. People were standing in line at the basement
door of the church. They were waiting for their turns
to be fed. Mahalia hurried to the side entrance.
Robert, Wilbur, Prince, and Louise were already

behind the steam table. Mahalia threw off her coat and joined them.

Mahalia knew that some of the church members went from store to market to solicit food from charitable storekeepers.

Some church members who owned small trucks delivered food stuffs to the church. Some cooked. Some washed dishes. No one expected money. They found this way to serve the Lord.

This night Mahalia felt especially hungry. Was it the nip in the air or was it the prospect of taking her first music lesson? She wondered.

She ate heartily when everyone was served, heaping her plate high with pigs' tails, sauerkraut, sweet potatoes, black-eyed beans, and bread pudding.

Prince talked while she ate. "What time are you two going to meet with the famous Professor?" he asked.

"Eight," answered Louise.

"I might as well go into the lion's den with plenty of food under my belt," said Mahalia, reaching for second helpings.

"I've heard you shouldn't eat before you sing," said Louise, "but knowing you, you'll do well full or empty."

Mahalia poised her fork mid-air, "I'm afraid. No one ever told me how to sing and I'm afraid I'm doing it all wrong."

After the hearty meal, the girls washed their faces, smoothed their hair, and prepared to meet Professor DuBois. Professor DuBois had a music salon on the South Side. They walked to his establishment.

When they arrived, they sat on the upholstered chairs in the waiting room. They could hear a soprano wailing toward high C.

As the soprano left, Professor DuBois came to greet

them. He was a tall, light-skinned Negro who had a
grand way about him. He was proud of his career as
a concert and operatic singer, and he told the girls so.

"Come in, come in," he said, inviting them to
precede him. He bowed slightly as they passed.

Mahalia felt uncomfortable with this man. His bow-
ing, his stilted voice, and his self-satisfied manner gave
her the feeling that she would never please him.

"Well, well, well," said the professor as he seated
himself at the piano. "So you need vocal lessons. We
shall see what we shall see."

"Here," the professor continued, "let me hear you
sing a spiritual." He handed her some sheet music.
The title was "Standing in the Need of Prayer."
Mahalia had sung it many times.

"I sang this a lot of times at the Mount Moriah
Baptist Church in New Orleans," Mahalia told the
Professor.

"Uhuh," he frowned. "That's the trouble with
blacks. You can get them out of the South, but you
can't get the South out of them. They just want to
sing what's familiar to them and not even try to ex-
pand their horizons."

Mahalia felt shaken. He hasn't even heard me yet
and he doesn't like me already, she thought.

She did not know how to read music, but she did
know the song. She watched the professor's hands as
they touched the keys. She thought hard about the
words and the music. The professor began playing.
Mahalia sang "It's me, it's me, it's me, O Lawd . . ."

The professor shook his head and dropped his hands
on the keyboard with a bang.

"That's no way to sing that song," he said. "Slow
down. Sing it like this."

He folded his hands together as if in prayer and
sang sadly and solemnly.

"See what I mean?" he asked. His hands went back to the keyboard.

Mahalia had such rhythm inside that she kept picking up the beat. As she did, she could see the professor frowning.

"No, No!" the professor said, raising his hand to stop her. "Now listen to the way I do it. This is the proper way." He sang a few more lines slowly, as if this spiritual was a funeral march. "Now try it my way, Miss Jackson."

Mahalia tried. It was no use. Mahalia could not hold back the joy she felt when singing.

The professor leaped from the piano stool. "You don't sing, you holler! It would take a long, long time to teach you to sing!"

Professor DuBois turned to Louise and said, "You try it."

Louise sang slowly, just the way the professor wanted her to.

"Now that's singing!" he exclaimed. "You have great possibilities."

Turning to Mahalia he said, "And you've got to learn to stop hollering. It will take time to teach you to breathe from the diaphragm, round your vowels, and stand with poise."

Mahalia felt all mixed up. Did she want to sing songs in a formal way? Would learning technique from Professor DuBois take away all the joy of singing for the Lord? Did the Lord really care if she stood a certain way? Wouldn't the Lord want her to sing from her heart, not her diaphragm?

Mahalia gave the professor her four dollars, then she and Louise left the salon.

"Wasn't he wonderful?" exclaimed Louise as they went down the stairs. "I'm going to take some more lessons."

"Not me," Mahalia said. "I don't want to sing none of that high class music. I'm never going back. I just want to sing like the Lord gave me to sing."

As the weeks wore by, Mahalia learned that not all the young people in the Johnson group cared as much about gospel singing as she did. After a while Mahalia was going off to sing by herself. She felt her singing was getting better, and sometimes she earned as much as ten dollars a week singing at funeral parlors and at churches.

By the middle of the Depression she was traveling outside Chicago. She sang at Negro churches all the way from New York to California.

Gospel music was gaining in popularity. It was the kind of music black people had left behind in the South and they loved it because it was like a letter from home.

Once, when she came back from a long singing trip, she found she had lost her laundry jobs. The white families on the North Side needed regular help and Mahalia was no longer regular.

"I don't know what to do," Mahalia told one of her church friends.

"Come around the place where I work," the girl told her. "The man will give you a job packing dates."

"I don't know anything about packing dates!" Mahalia exclaimed.

"You don't have to know anything," the girl answered. "You just sit there and the dates come to you and you put them in a box."

Mahalia applied at the date plant on the West Side of the city. She agreed to work for seven dollars a week. They gave her a blue uniform and sat her beside a big moving belt. Date boxes came shooting by and she put the dates in each box as it went by.

Mahalia did not make friends with any of the girls who worked at the date plant. They were not like the church girls she knew. They said mean things to each other and were always threatening each other with fights.

Then, one afternoon, as the girls were changing out of their uniforms at the end of the shift, two girls began fighting. They pulled out long knives and screeched at each other. The others ran out as fast as they could.

Mahalia never went back to the date plant. She was fortunate enough to get a maid's job just a few days later. It was in a big hotel where she cleaned thirty-three rooms every day for twelve dollars a week.

Then the Decca recording company's South Side studio asked her to record, "God's Gonna Separate the Wheat from the Tares," a song she had often sung. Only three years after Professor DuBois told her she couldn't sing, she was asked to do a recording!

It was 1934, the fifth year of the Great Depression, and she was going to get twenty-five dollars for a recording! Well, she knew one thing she would do with the money. She'd pay for Grandpa Paul Clark to travel north from New Orleans and visit them.

9

Grandfather Paul and a Vow and a Husband

Mahalia felt a little guilty taking twenty-five dollars for singing a song she loved. But she told herself that this was business. Black artists were making many records for black listeners. Mahalia knew that salesmen would go door to door with her record, selling it to black people who had none of the proper conveniences in their homes, but who would get enough money to buy a phonograph and records. They liked the records best that were made by black musicians and black singers.

It was exciting to have Grandpa Paul here this summer. He was her mother's father. Grandpa had been born a slave on a cotton plantation in Louisiana. He always enjoyed telling about life in the log cabin where his fifteen children were born. For a man of seventy-eight, his memory was good.

Mahalia let herself into the apartment and stood for a moment to enjoy looking at the old man sitting at the head of the table. To her he looked like royalty surrounded by his adoring subjects.

When she came into the dining room there was a great round of "hello's" and laughter.

"Isn't it wonderful to have Grandpa Paul with us!" Mahalia exclaimed.

And then it came to her that this was such a memorable occasion that they should all go to the photographer around the corner and have their picture taken with Grandpa Paul in the middle.

"That's a good idea," Aunt Alice said.

"Maybe not," mused Mahalia.

"What do you mean?" asked Aunt Hannah.

"Maybe all we need is a picture of Grandpa alone."

Mahalia realized the big decision was how to get Grandpa away from the table before he took a nap right there on the spot.

While Mahalia hurried to serve the blackberry cobbler, she kept talking.

"Grandpa," she said, "I think it would be awfully nice if you would come to the photographer's with me and have your picture taken. It will give us something to keep forever when you go back to New Orleans."

"It's too hot for him to go out after eating," Hannah said.

"It won't take very long," said Mahalia.

"Where's all the money coming from?" asked Alice. "Pictures ain't cheap."

"I've got a little money," said Mahalia.

"Tell you what I'll do. If you sing my favorite song, I'll go with you to the photographer's," Grandpa Paul said.

Mahalia knew his favorite song. She stood up and began to sing.

> Steal away, steal away,
> Steal away to Jesus,
> Steal away, steal away home,
> I ain't got long to stay here.

Finally Mahalia routed them out of the apartment and to the photographer's.

"What'd you want a picture of me for?" Grandpa Paul argued as he walked along. "An ugly old man like me ain't for takin' pictures of!"

It was a hot day and the old man kept wiping his forehead with a red bandana.

The photographer got Grandpa Paul to put his bandana away and sit on a comfortable chair in front of the camera. Grandpa's eyes began to roll. He leaned far to the left. Then he slid out of the chair and onto the floor. His eyes were closed and he lay still, very still.

"Oh!" cried Mahalia, "Grandpa! Grandpa!" She rushed to raise him off the floor, but the photographer pushed her aside.

"Don't touch him," he said in a commanding voice. "Someone call an ambulance."

In a short time the ambulance was there and orderlies hurried to put Grandpa on a stretcher and rush him to the hospital.

Mahalia and Aunt Hannah hailed a taxi. The others followed in a second taxi.

When they got to the hospital the doctors had already examined the old man.

"Is he going to be all right?" Mahalia asked breathlessly.

"We don't know," a young doctor said, shaking his head sadly. "We're not sure he'll last through the night. Perhaps you had better stay."

Aunt Hannah was sobbing with fear and grief. She turned her tear-streaked face toward Mahalia. "If you hadn't sent Papa out into this terrible heat," she said, "this never would have happened. His death is going to be on your shoulders!"

Aunt Hannah's words cut into Mahalia like an alligator gnashing its teeth against her insides. She turned and walked down the hall. Surely she loved her grandfather as much as anyone. Mahalia entered an empty room and fell to her knees. Tears flowed down her cheeks. Was it all her fault? Was it? Would this not have happened if she had let him nap after his dinner?

If God would only let him live so that she would not spend the rest of her life feeling she had killed him!

A prayer formed on her lips. "Oh, Lord," she prayed, "if You will only let Grandfather live, I will make the rest of my life as pure as I can."

Mahalia tried to think of something that would be

a sacrifice for her. She enjoyed motion pictures and vaudeville shows.

"Dear Lord," Mahalia prayed, "if you will make Grandfather well, I will never go to another theater again."

She made the same vow again and again for the next nine days. On the ninth day her grandfather was better. He walked out of the hospital well and strong. He returned to his home in the South where he lived for some years afterward.

Mahalia was happy once again and could continue with her church work and her singing.

Mahalia thought her life had fallen into a routine pattern until one day, during a church social, she met a man who had come to hear the Johnson Gospel Singers. He was a graduate of Fisk University and Tuskegee Institute. He had studied to be a chemist, but in 1935 the only job he could get in Chicago was as a mail carrier for the Post Office. His name was Isaac Hockenhull.

They talked together easily. Mahalia learned he was 34, ten years older than she!

Ike walked Mahalia home the night they met and for many nights after that. They went together for a year. They fell in love and wanted to marry. Mahalia worried about money. She wasn't making much as a hotel maid and had only a few singing engagements. Ike was an extra at the Post Office and his income was slight.

They were married in Aunt Hannah's apartment by the pastor of Greater Salem Baptist Church. They moved in with Aunt Hannah, Alice, Nathaniel, and the roomer. This was not a comfortable arrangement. One of the happenings that caused conflict was Ike's locking himself in the only bathroom to experiment with making cosmetics and hair ointments. Ike

explained to all that as soon as he perfected these
cosmetics, he planned to have Mahalia sell them at
the places where she had her singing engagements.

Finally, Mahalia could not stand the constant conflict between her husband and her relatives, so she
decided that they should have an apartment of their
own. Ike agreed. ''Money from the sale of my
cosmetics will make this entirely possible,'' he told
Mahalia.

Mahalia found out something else about Ike. She
learned that he spent a great deal of time at the public
library.

''Why?'' she asked him.

''I want to learn the pedigrees, speed, and en-
durance of race horses,'' Ike answered.

Now Mahalia knew Ike's great weakness. It was
betting on horses! How could she have been so blind?
How could she not have known that her husband was

a gambler? Mahalia decided everything would be all right. She would pray for him.

She tried to make their money take care of their needs. Often they stayed up all night making dozens of jars of cosmetics. Mahalia always took a suitcase full when she went on the road, and sold out at gospel meetings where she sang.

But Ike was not content. He wanted Mahalia to take voice lessons. He wanted her to be a concert singer.

"Why do you want to waste your wonderful voice on that stuff?" he asked many times.

Mahalia told him gospel singing was a part of her. She loved it.

"The Lord gave me my voice," Mahalia would say. "I want to use it to praise Him."

She would not give in. Ike would not stop arguing with her about it.

Once Ike showed her a clipping about tryouts for the "Hot Mikado," a jazzed up version of an operetta. The rent was past due. They had been eating beans and rice for a week.

Finally she went to the tryouts. "I promised God I wouldn't go to the theater," she thought. "I don't think I should sing in one either."

Someone called Mahalia's name. She forced herself to the stage. She sang, "Sometimes I Feel Like a Motherless Chile." Mahalia saw the three men who were hiring people talking together. She could tell they liked her. She hurried off stage as the next singer took her place.

When she got home Ike opened the door. He was smiling. "You got the part. They just called from the theater and said to tell you that you got the part."

"Oh," was all Mahalia said.

"I got a job today, too," Ike said.

"Then I don't have to sing jazz. I don't want to be in that show," Mahalia said.

Ike looked as if he would blow up and burst. Then he found his voice and boomed his objections. He pleaded. He argued.

"All I want to do is sing for the Lord," Mahalia said quietly.

Mahalia and Ike had a "sandpaper" relationship after their disagreement about gospel singing.

Mahalia said, "When you have something deep inside you, when you're torn apart by it, when you've got to express what's inside of you for the world, nothing can stop you."

The marriage eventually ended in divorce, and Mahalia felt more emptiness than at any time since her mother's death. She carried the hurt inside her for many years, while outwardly she bravely faced her responsibilities.

10

Beautician, Florist
Song Plugger

By the time the Depression was over in the late thirties, Mahalia was earning enough from her singing to keep her away from maid's work. She was not sure she could always make a living by her singing, so she decided to take the money she had saved and learn to be a beautician. It was not fulfilling her dream to become a nurse, but it was giving people a service.

She went to the Scott Institute of Beauty Culture to learn to become a hairdresser. By 1939 she had saved enough to buy the equipment for a beauty parlor. She called her shop "Mahalia's Beauty Salon." Many customers came to the shop because they knew Mahalia through the church and because of her singing. Soon Mahalia had five girls working for her.

These were busy days for Mahalia. On weekends she traveled to churches in St. Louis and Detroit and many other towns, and then she hurried back to her hairdressing business.

Mahalia was so encouraged by her success at the beauty business that she decided to branch out and try still another business for which she felt there was a need. She studied floral design and opened a shop called ''Mahalia's House of Flowers.'' Her florist business did well. People were always asking her to sing at funerals, and many of them bought their flowers from Mahalia.

Mahalia was glad she had her shops and her music to keep her busy. She was living alone now.

Then one evening after choir practice Thomas A. Dorsey, the black composer, came to Greater Salem Baptist Church to offer Mahalia a song plugger's job. It was the spring of 1939. Mahalia was suspicious of some people. Her gospel recordings had earned her hundreds of dollars but they had been stolen from her. The records, ''God's Gonna Separate the Wheat From the Tares,'' ''Keep Me Every Day,'' and ''God Will Wipe All Tears Away,'' had been copied without her permission. They sold well. But Mahalia did not profit from these stolen songs.

Mahalia listened to Dorsey with suspicion. She wanted to know what a song plugger did. Dorsey explained that a song plugger was a singer hired to sing a composer's songs and try to get people to buy them.

Mahalia wanted to know more about Dorsey before she would decide to take the job. She found out that he was the son of a Baptist preacher and that he was the composer of the gospel hit, ''If You See My Savior, Tell Him that You Saw Me.'' Mahalia listened while Dorsey talked about the bright future for gospel music.

Mahalia finally agreed to be a song plugger. Her

first job was to be in Springfield, Illinois. Dorsey hired an old gospel singer, Bob Jones. Bob Jones had lost his voice and needed work. The three of them headed south from Chicago. Their tank was full of gas. They also carried an emergency supply of gas and oil in case they ran out and a white filling-station attendant chose not to sell them fuel. That sometimes happened to black people. Mahalia, always concerned with food, made sandwiches and a big thermos of coffee, so they wouldn't have to go to the rear of restaurants to buy food.

When they came to the little Baptist church in Springfield, Mahalia realized the church was too poor to pay them much. Why, she could even see the basement through the cracks in the floor!

She heard Dorsey talking to the pastor. He was saying, "I have to admire Mahalia though we don't always agree on the way she sings my songs. She's big and forceful and fiery. Her talent is overpowering. She breaks all the rules, changes melody and meter as the spirit moves her. She sings to that mysterious inner beat."

Mahalia smiled at his speech. And when she finished singing to that congregation, the audience's "Thank You, Jesus," repeated over and over again took more than half an hour.

Mahalia worked and sang for years before she made her big record. She was thirty-five years old. The true story of the song that made her famous may never be known. There are several versions. According to one of the most popular accounts, a black gospel composer, a competitor of Dorsey, the Reverend W. Herbert Brewster, wrote the song. But Mahalia said she had been singing the song since she was a child, long before Brewster composed it. The song was entitled, "I Will Move On Up a Little Higher."

A man from Decca Records, named Ink Williams, heard Mahalia sing the song, asked her to make a record of it, and distributed the record all over the United States. The record sold almost two million copies.

"Movin' On Up" made Mahalia famous with Negroes. She was still practically unknown to whites until 1950. One day Mahalia got a letter from a man named Marshall Stearns. Mr. Stearns taught music at the New School for Social Research in New York. Mr. Stearns was planning a symposium (a meeting for the discussion on a specific subject) on the origins of jazz music. This meeting was going to be held at a place called Music Inn up in the Berkshires in Massachusetts. Music professors from the Juilliard School of Music and many other notable institutions were invited to the symposium to talk and study about folk music and jazz.

Mr. Stearns explained that he knew Mahalia's voice from the record, "Movin' On Up," and he wanted her to come to Massachusetts and sing gospel songs for those attending this symposium.

Mahalia found out that Music Inn was not far from Tanglewood, where summer festivals of classical music took place. The Inn was a big old estate that Philip Barber and his wife, Stephanie, had bought and fixed up so that people could come there to study jazz and classical music, or just relax and listen to music.

When Mahalia arrived, they were still remodeling the Music Inn. They gave Mahalia an old horse stall to sleep in. She told the young man who helped her with her bags, "I finally made it into the white folks' world and look where it landed me!"

Mahalia was treated to a delicious supper after which Marshall Stearns asked the music professors to gather in the old carriage house, which had been made into a lounge. A new baby grand piano sat at the east end of the room.

Mahalia smiled, walked to the piano, and, leaning on the instrument, sang. She sang "Didn't it Rain, Lord!" and "Jesus, Savior, Pilot Me" and "Movin' On Up."

She seemed to be singing directly to God. Her voice, her attitude, her gestures praised God with deep love and warmth and joy. The people gathered there that evening felt caught up in her great outpouring of faith.

"Where did you learn to sing in that manner?" one teacher asked.

"No one taught me," Mahalia answered. "I sing exactly the way I feel."

Then all the other teachers and professors began to ply her with questions. "What is gospel?" "Where did it come from?"

"From my people," Mahalia explained. "To make their lives a little more bearable when they were slaves. They sang as they worked. The songs they made up were sad songs, but they told of a better life to come."

Mahalia went on, "When they were freed from slavery, their songs were happier. They were sure that life was going to get better for them. These songs were called 'jubilees'. Gospel has some of both spirituals and jubilees in it."

Mahalia told the group that she'd been singing at Baptist churches and gospel tents and prayer meetings all her life because she loved singing, and black people liked to hear her sing. She told the professors that she had had one music lesson. She explained how she didn't learn to sing any special way. She just found herself doing it.

The teachers asked Mahalia to sing again and

again. They got out their tape recorders and played some African bongo music and asked her if that sounded familiar.

"I don't know anything about jungle drums, but the beat sounds good," Mahalia told them. "It really does something for me."

Mahalia stayed a whole week at Music Inn. She knew she moved them with her songs. She was sure she did when expert Philip Barber told her, "Mahalia, if you'd started out the door and down to the lake while you were singing, 'Shall We Gather at the River,' all of us would have followed you and waded right into the water to be baptized."

Carnegie Hall

The experts at Music Inn agreed that Mahalia had preserved black singing. Despite all the people who wanted her to sing like whites, Mahalia had kept the faith in black music. She had indeed enriched the treasury of black American song.

Mahalia decided that it was time she had her own accompanist. She knew she didn't need much music to back up her voice. In fact she preferred singing by herself. Often pianists who followed music to the note couldn't understand her variations. But, she reasoned, a pianist helped if that pianist knew Mahalia was calling the tune, and knew how Mahalia felt about what she was to sing at the moment. Happily, Mildred Falls and Mahalia became acquainted at this time. Mildred knew just what Mahalia wanted. Mildred could write songs, too. She began playing for Mahalia and stayed with her to the end.

Everything began happening at once after the professors from the symposium went back home and

started telling people in the churches and in the concert field about Mahalia.

Once back in Chicago, she received many invitations to sing. She appeared on a coast-to-coast television show. It was the most popular show of the times,
called the Ed Sullivan Show. She was made the official
soloist for the National Baptist Convention, the largest
Negro church group in the world.

Then came an invitation that made Mahalia's head
spin. Joe Bostic phoned Mahalia. He was a brilliant
black disc jockey and gospel promoter who arranged
concerts and had been partially responsible for having Mahalia invited to the symposium at Music Inn.

"Will you sing in New York?" he asked.

"Sure," Mahalia replied.

To her, New York meant Harlem or one of the big
Baptist churches in Brooklyn.

"Good!" Joe said. "I'm booking you for Carnegie
Hall."

There was a long pause.

"You mean Carnegie Hall on Fifty-seventh Street
where the great ones perform?" Mahalia asked.

Mildred Falls laughed, and taking the phone out
of the astonished Mahalia's hand, said, "I'm not
afraid to play at Carnegie Hall. Even though there
are two thousand seven hundred and eighty-four seats
in the place, I'm not afraid."

"Hush, Mildred," said Mahalia. "One fool at a
time."

Joe Bostic went on talking, telling her the session
at Music Inn had started all the experts talking about
her. "Besides, New York is where your talent gets
measured. New York has the critics, the magazines,
and the newspapers to tell everybody about Mahalia
Jackson."

"Will all those high class people understand my songs?" Mahalia asked.

"God moves in mysterious ways His wonders to perform," said Joe.

"Maybe gospel will break down the color line," said Mildred.

This convinced Mahalia. "I'll do it!" she told Joe.

On the night of the concert, when Mahalia walked onto the stage, she breathed out in surprise. Every seat in the huge hall was filled.

It was said afterward that the music critic of the *New York Times*, who went to Carnegie Hall that night, thought he'd gotten caught in a Cecil B. DeMille mob scene. It was a Negro mob scene.

The crowd around Carnegie Hall was so big that midtown traffic was all tied up. Inside, people swarmed up and down the aisles and up to the top seats in the balconies. The box office sold out the last standing room and put people up on the stage. When it was time for Mahalia to sing, there was just a little space left for her to stand next to the piano.

Mahalia gazed at the thousands of men and women who had come to hear her, everyday people—baby nurse, wash woman, factory worker. She was overcome by the knowledge that she was standing on the same stage where great artists like Caruso, Lily Pons, and Marian Anderson had performed. She clutched her throat. Would she be able to utter a sound?

Black people had come down from Harlem. Some had traveled from as far away as Baltimore and Philadelphia and Boston.

She began to sing.

> Just as I am, without one plea
> But that thy blood was shed for me,
> And that Thou bid'st me come to thee.
> Oh, Lamb of God, I come, I come.

The more Mahalia sang, the more the people cried out for joy. People began shouting all over the great hall. Toes tapped and hands waved. Some people got up to dance. Many in the audience cried unashamedly.

Mahalia got more and more into the spirit of the performance and went down on her knees. But she soon straightened up and said, "Now we'd best remember we're in Carnegie Hall, and if we cut up too much, they might put us out."

The records of attendance set by Arturo Toscanini and Benny Goodman concerts were broken. Rave reviews appeared in the newspapers. Mahalia was a success!

When it was all over, Mahalia sank wearily into a chair backstage. "Just think, Mildred," she said, "me a black washerwoman from the South singing in Carnegie Hall. The Lord be praised!"

By 1950 Mahalia was earning fifty thousand dollars a year from her singing. She could hardly believe it. Besides her income from concert tours, radio, television, and recordings, she was getting huge offers from nightclub and jazz band leaders. These she refused, explaining that she had made a vow in 1934 never to sing where whiskey was sold. The nightclubs promised her they would not serve whiskey while she sang. Still she refused.

Mahalia continued to serve God. She enjoyed the boys and girls in her neighborhood and invited them into her apartment to hear Bible stories. They sat on the floor and listened as she read aloud from her Bible.

One day she announced to the children, "I will give a Christmas surprise to everyone who goes to Sunday school!" This was her way of being a missionary to those around her.

Mahalia lived simply, saving her money because

"success was too good to last." She could never forget the bad times. Her only luxury was a Cadillac in which she lived when touring sections of America where a black with a million dollars did not have enough money to buy an unsegregated glass of water.

These days were confusing to Mahalia. She put it this way. "It's not that I think I'm a special black. Not at all. I don't expect to be treated better than any other black. It's just when I move back and forth between the white and black world every day, the stupidity and cruelty of Jim Crow hurts. It hits you so hard you don't know whether to explode with anger or stay on your knees praying for understanding, praying for whites and blacks to get hatred out of their hearts so they can get on with the business of living. While on the concert stage or in the TV studio white people say they love me. On the street they ignore me."

Then Mahalia gave a series of concerts to raise money for her church, the Greater Salem Baptist. It was used to build an extension to the recreation room and to send children from the South Side's hot streets to summer camp.

Mahalia put aside money to take care of needy members of her own family, enlarged now by members of her father's second family, and the aunts, uncles, and cousins who had come to Chicago.

Then, following her success on television, she learned that the French Academy of Music had honored her recording of "I Can Put My Trust in Jesus" with an award. Would she come to France to receive it?

Her fans in Europe made it plain that if she came to France she should give them a chance to hear her. Many countries, including England, Holland, Belgium, and Denmark, made it clear that they wanted to hear Mahalia Jackson sing.

"I hate to travel," Mahalia told Mildred. "I'm really afraid to fly. Ships make me sick to my stomach."

"Do you want to bring gospel music to Europe?" Mildred asked. Mildred knew just how to change Mahalia's mind.

They planned a whirlwind trip to Europe, and soon Mahalia and Mildred flew to England.

"This will be one country who will like us," Mahalia said. "At least they understand the language. They'll know what I'm singing about."

The English came to the concerts in Cambridge and London. They were not carried away with Mahalia's singing. It was hard to tell who was more disappointed, Mahalia or the English. There was a cool response to her singing. Almost no one clapped. There was an embarrassed silence after her performances.

Mahalia was flabbergasted. "Dear Lord," she prayed, "give my the strength and the heart to finish this European tour."

When she and Mildred got to Paris they had to call out the police to hold back the crowd. Even though the French could not understand the words, they were filled with such religious feeling that many wept during the concerts.

The women went on to Holland, Belgium, and Denmark. The morning after a concert in Copenhagen, children filled the hotel lobby with flowers. In the next few days, people ordered fifty thousand copies of Mahalia's record, "Silent Night."

Mahalia knew that Europe was certainly in her future again, but first she wanted to plant her roots in Chicago. She was sure the North was where her permanent roots should be, because here the Negroes were free.

Mahalia had an apartment in Chicago, but she dreamed of having a home with trees and grass and maybe a garden. Mahalia dreamed of a place of her own every time she went on tour and spent her leisure hours in hotel rooms. She wanted a well-equipped kitchen where she could cook all her specialities.

When Mahalia sang in St. Louis, Missouri, she stayed with her friend Genese Smith, who was another gospel singer. One night they were sitting at the kitchen table singing and humming religious songs when the landlady ran up the stairs and pounded with hammer-like strokes on Genese's door.

"Why don't you go to bed?" she screamed. "People don't want to hear your yowling in the middle of the night."

"I'm sorry, Mahalia," Genese apologized.

"Don't let it worry you, honey," Mahalia said. "I rent, too, and they do the same to me back in my apartment in Chicago. But one of these days I'm gonna own the whole apartment house and I'll be able to holler as loud as I like."

When Mahalia returned to Chicago, she did find an apartment house to buy.

"It will be a good investment for you," the real estate agent told her.

Mahalia thought she now had more freedom to live as she pleased, but it did not work out that way. One day she was singing in the full power of her voice when a tenant pounded on her door.

"Yes?" asked Mahalia as she opened the door.

"We pay our rent on time," the woman said. Her eyes bulged and her voice squeaked with rage. "We have every right to expect a little peace and quiet for our money!"

"Yes," Mahalia said.

Letters came from her fans. Chicago's Poles,

Czechs, Yogoslavs, Ukrainians, Germans, Scandinavians, Irish, Italians, Jews, as well as blacks, wrote warm, friendly letters. Her show's producer, who was Jewish, persuaded her to sing songs dear to his people. Her Irish sponsor got her to sing his people's songs.

The half-hour show was later purchased by a TV distributor and sold to stations throughout the country.

In 1954 the sweeping decision by the Supreme Court outlawing racial segregation in the public schools became the law of the land. Mahalia was hopeful that whites and blacks could live peacefully.

She started looking for a new home. After Mahalia had covered the Chicago suburbs without success, she went to a real estate agent.

"When I ask the price of a house where there is a 'for sale' sign," Mahalia explained, "people slam the door in my face. They say they've changed their minds and are not going to sell."

The agent made use of Mahalia's reputation, advertising for someone to sell a home to Mahalia Jackson, "the Gospel Queen." A white dentist, a fan of Mahalia's replied. "I'll be proud to sell my house to Mahalia," he said.

But the people in the neighborhood didn't feel as the dentist did. The eight-room, red brick, ranch-style house with picture window and California patio was too elegant for a black, some said. Some of the neighbors believed that if they let Mahalia live in peace, other black families would move in, too. Rumors spread that Mahalia had ten children, all school age. What terrible things would happen to their schools with all those black children interfering with the established routine? With other blacks moving into the neighborhood, the value of the homes there would go down.

While her decorators were placing the furniture and antiques in her new home, the phone began ringing. Callers would say, ''Wait and see what we'll do to you. We're going to blow you away with dynamite. Your God won't save you.''

When phone threats did not drive her out, bullets were shot into her windows. She was afraid to turn on the lights at night. She went to the police for protection. They guarded her house day and night. She almost took her friends' advice about moving out when her gaze fell on the framed quotation on her living room wall: ''Dear Lord in this House You Are Wanted and You Are Welcome.''

''The Lord is on the side of Right,'' Mahalia said. ''I'm going to stick it out.''

One day Mildred came over for another practice session. Mahilia was grateful that they could now practice as long and as loudly as they pleased.

Rosa Parks and Dr. King

Mahalia noticed one day in early December that Mildred was thinking inward thoughts. Serious thoughts.

"What's on your mind that makes you stare out the window with frowns and sighs?" asked Mahalia.

"Have you read what happened in Montgomery, Alabama, on December first?" Mildred answered Mahalia's question with a question.

"I did read about a Mrs. Parks who wouldn't give up her seat," Mahalia answered.

Mildred strode to the hall closet and got her purse. She extracted a paper. "Let me read you this account of what happened and then you'll know why I'm so concerned.

Mildred began reading. "Mrs. Rosa Parks, a black seamstress, has been brought to trial in Montgomery, Alabama. The reason for the arrest was given as a broken Jim Crow law. Mrs. Parks refused to move out of her seat in the Negro section of a Cleveland Avenue city bus so that a white man could sit down.''

Mahalia sighed. "There is trouble," she said.

A short time later Mildred came to Mahalia's house again. "I'm really not in the mood for practice," she said. "I've brought over this article. Let me read it aloud to you and see what you think.''

Mildred cleared her throat and began to read.

"Arresting Rosa Parks turned out to be a spark that might set fire to a big dispute. There were about fifty thousand colored people in Montgomery and the day when they brought Mrs. Parks to trial about twenty-five thousand Negroes refused to ride on city buses by way of protest. The next day about ninety percent of the Negroes in that city had joined in the bus boycott.

"Young Negro ministers led by Martin Luther King, Jr., had joined together to lead the way. They organized the Montgomery Improvement Association with the Reverend Abernathy as President. They worked through the colored churches to raise money to get car pools organized so that Negroes could get to their jobs.''

Mahalia shook her head and frowned. "These are troubled times," she told Mildred. "But it just had to come. All Americans must learn to live together.''

Mahalia and Mildred went on with their practicing, but they watched television, listened to the radio, and read Chicago papers and the Montgomery papers, too.

They learned what Dr. King was saying. He said, "Walk straight. Walk the streets of Montgomery until the walls of segregation are battered by the forces of justice.''

They read that Dr. King preached courage to Montgomery's fifty thousand Negroes. The bus boycott became a walking, praying crusade.

Dr. King patterned the crusade after Gandhi's nonviolent movement in India. The papers quoted him as saying, "I used the teachings of Jesus to give spirit to the movement. I used the methods learned from Gandhi and Thoreau."

Dr. King spoke to his people in terms he knew they could understand. He knew the Negro race had a long and deep religious faith. He said things like, "Our weapon is love. Hate cannot drive out hate. Only love can do that."

Mahalia agreed with Dr. King. He was saying the phrases she had sung so many times!

Mahalia understood that he was teaching the true meanings of nonviolent resistance. The movement was not against persons, but against the system of discrimination.

"You must be willing to suffer the penalty for your resistance," he said. "Above all, you must be willing to go on loving those who make you suffer."

One night while the boycott was in full force, Dr. King spoke at a church meeting. Terrible news came to him as he spoke.

Mahalia read all about it. It was reported that in the middle of Dr. King's speech, a person ran up to him and announced in a loud voice, "Your house has been bombed!"

"Are my wife and baby all right?" Dr. King asked.

"We're not sure. That is being checked now," came the reply.

The article said that Dr. King rushed home. The bomb had damaged a part of the porch and had shattered the windows. Inside, the Mayor of Montgomery and other Montgomery officials were checking out the scene. They assured Dr. King that his wife, Coretta, and his daughter, Yoki, were not harmed.

But outside the King home, more than one thousand Negroes had gathered. They were ready for violent retaliation.

"Vengeance!" some shouted.

Dr. King faced the angry mob. He could see they were ready to rip into the city of Montgomery and tear it to shreads. He raised his arm. "If you have weapons, take them home," he said.

His face was sad. "We must meet hate with love. Leave peacefully. God is with this movement."

The crowd became silent. They saw their leader's teachings in action. His wife and baby could have been killed. Yet he talked about love.

A young man moved forward. "God bless you, Dr. King!" he shouted. The crowd moved away.

It was a surprise to Mahalia to get a letter from Dr. King asking if she could come down to Montgomery to sing at a rally to raise some money. After all she had heard, seen, and read about the Montgomery Improvement Association, Mahalia did not hesitate to accept the invitation.

"Will you go with me?" she asked Mildred.

"I'd feel hurt if you hadn't asked me," replied Mildred.

Mahalia was happy to meet the Reverend Abernathy, whom she thought was a brave young man. She was surprised that Dr. Martin Luther King, Jr. was not a big man.

"His spirit is big, though," she confided to Mildred.

Mahalia and Mildred were invited to stay at the Abernathys'.

"It's just a little white frame house, but its ours and we love it," Mrs. Abernathy said.

The Abernathys' gave up their own beds for

Mahalia and Mildred. Mrs. Abernathy cooked a good supper of greens, corn bread, and ham hocks.

"Let us pray together," the Reverend Abernathy said after supper.

When they bowed their heads he prayed, "Almighty God, Eternal Spirit, we, for whom Thou art the only hope of our people, acknowledge our need of Thee now. Amen."

They left for the rally at the Methodist Church in Montgomery. They chose this church because it was the biggest in the city.

Police were all around. Cars full of white men drove up. They called out and threw rocks and bottles, but they could not stop the rally. Ministers spoke. Milling crowds outside the church listened to loudspeakers, while the overflow crowds in the church were orderly and attentive.

When it was time for Mahalia to sing, she stood up and looked at Mildred. Mildred moved quickly to the piano. Instinctively she knew what to play. The song was, "Move On Up a Little Higher." When Mahalia sang, the segregationists who had come to cause commotion were silent. Then Mahalia sang, "Walk Together, Children, Don't You Get Weary."

Dr. King stood by the pulpit and began his sermon. Mahalia knew he was only twenty-seven years old, which was young for such an influential leader. This small man had a certain strength. His father was an outstanding minister in Atlanta, Georgia. His grandfather, too, had been a preacher whom people looked up to.

Dr. King was saying blacks should not hate their enemies. Turn the other cheek. Hate drains off one's energy and blacks needed all their energy. Meet violence with nonviolence was what Dr. King was advocating. Mahalia listened to Dr. King. She felt uplifted and hopeful and prayerful.

Mahalia knew she and Dr. King were much alike in many ways. Dr. King had sung solos in church when his father was pastor of the Ebenezer Baptist Church on Auburn Avenue in Atlanta. His mother played the organ and directed the church choir. Martin Luther King grew up loving words as well as songs.

The King children grew up knowing love. A sister, Willie Christine, was a year older than Martin. Alfred Daniel (called A.D.) was a year younger. The children ran to Grandmother Jennie when things went wrong. Martin adored his grandmother, who was always able to console him with a kiss or a cheery word.

"There's nothing more important than loving one another," she told the King children.

Mahalia's attention went back to what Dr. King was saying.

"We are tired—tired of being segregated and humiliated; tired of being kicked about by the brutal feet of opression. For many years we have shown amazing patience. Love must be our regulating ideal."

Mahalia decided that she could do more for her people than just sing at rallies. She made a solemn vow to herself. She promised herself that she would give a considerable part of her money to support Dr. King's work to bring equal rights to blacks.

Mahalia felt that she was part of something so important that it would go down in history.

It did not surprise her to read in one of the newspapers, "Montgomery is a legend that was written by cooks, janitors, and country people."

Black people everywhere had a new leader.

Dr. Ralph Abernathy's dedication to rights for blacks was felt everywhere, too. A story went around in the South that Dr. Abernathy met an old Negro woman walking down a road on the way to work. Buses passed her, but she refused to ride.

"Aren't you too tired to walk a long distance every day?" Abernathy asked.

"Before, my soul was tired. Now, only my feet are tired, because my soul has found peace."

Abernathy smiled. His labors were bearing fruit.

Abernathy grew up in Marengo County, in the heart of Alabama's Black Belt. This is where his parents owned a five hundred acre farm.

He was ordained a Baptist minister in 1948, received a B.S. from Alabama State College in 1950 and an M.A. from Atlanta University in 1951. In that year Abernathy was named pastor of the First Baptist Church in Montgomery, Alabama. It was during this time that he developed a close friendship with Dr. King.

After the rally, Mahalia and Mildred left Montgomery. The next night the bedroom that she and Mildred had occupied in the Abernathy home was leveled to the ground with dynamite. The Abernathys escaped without injuries.

As time went on, Mrs. Abernathy wrote Mahalia that the bus lines were getting desperate for money. It was because of the boycott. They charged higher fares for white passengers, but they went deeper into debt.

Finally, the next year the Supreme Court handed down the verdict that segregation in buses was against the Constitution. But because the law was on the books did not mean everything would work out as the law said. President Eisenhower had to order Federal troops into Little Rock, Arkansas, to make sure that nine black children could enter Central High School. In Virginia, the whites of Prince Edward County decided to shut down the public schools rather than integrate them.

Then four black students in North Carolina decided

to do something that fired the sense of justice throughout the world. In 1960, they sat down at a lunch counter in Greensboro and ordered cups of coffee. The waiter refused to serve them coffee or anything else. He said that North Carolina law did not allow him to serve blacks. He sàid the men should know that, since they were students at North Carolina A & T College.

"We shall sit here until we are served," one man said. The others nodded.

They sat in the restaurant until the police came and took them away. They did not resist the police even when they were handled roughly. They believed in Martin Luther King's preaching of nonviolence and passive resistance.

In the next three weeks Mahalia read that the sit-in protest spread to fifteen cities in five states of the South. More than a thousand young people were arrested. They staged their sit-ins in public libraries (blacks had been denied the right to borrow books), at swimming pools, beaches, hotel lobbies, movie houses.

The protests moved north. Mahalia sent fifty thousand dollars to underwrite expenses in such places as Pittsburgh, Detroit, New York, and Washington.

Students continued to follow King's advice about nonviolence. They sat peacefully at counters while white hecklers poured catsup on their clothes and salt on their heads. In Orangeburg, South Carolina, police threw tear gas at students gathering outside a restaurant, and then firemen turned their hoses on the students. The tremendous force of the water knocked the students down. Then they were hauled off to jail.

King and his brother joined students in a sit-in at a department store in Atlanta. They were jailed with the students. King was sentenced to four months of hard labor at Reidsville State prison. The Justice Department pressured President Eisenhower to arrange for King's release, but the President did nothing.

It was an election year. Senator John Kennedy and Vice-President Nixon were the presidential candidates. Kennedy's brother, Robert, called the judge and asked about King's constitutional right to bail. John Kennedy called Mrs. King and offered his sympathy and support. The next day the judge granted King bail. King was free. The news spread. Senator Kennedy received the gratitude of the Negro population.

It was about this time, at a special student meeting in Raleigh, North Carolina, everyone joined hands and sang, "We Shall Overcome." This became the hymn of the movement.

The Star Spangled Banner

The 1960s would be crucial years for the nation. Were there chances for real peace? Above all, the new president, soon to be elected, would need to fathom Communist intentions. The new President would need to understand the Russians and particularly their leader Nikita S. Khrushchev.

Mahalia heard from Mrs. King that until now Dr. King's father had been cool toward Senator Kennedy. But he changed his mind.

He said, "This man was willing to wipe the tears from my daughter-in-law's eyes. I've got a suitcase full of votes and I'm going to take them to Mr. Kennedy and dump them in his lap."

Black votes began going for the Democrats. Mahalia heard that across the country seven out of ten Negro votes were believed to be cast for the Democrats.

The election excitement was just calming down

when Mahalia got a call from Hollywood, California. It was Peter Lawford, a motion picture actor. He explained that a big Inauguration gala celebration was being planned for President Kennedy. He invited Mahalia to sing "The Star Spangled Banner." This was to be the night before John F. Kennedy was to take the oath of office as president.

Mahalia sat by the phone trying to digest the thrilling invitation. Was it really true? Had she just received a call from someone asking her to sing in Washington, D.C.?

Her hand was still resting on the phone when it rang again.

"Is this Mahalia Jackson?" A man with a deep voice asked the question.

"Yes."

"This is Mayor Daley," the man said. "There will be a number of us going on my special train. We'd like to have you and your accompanist join us."

"Mayor Daley?"

"Yes."

"Of Chicago?"

"Yes."

"You talking about going to Washington, D.C., on a special train?" Mahalia asked. Her voice box felt as if it was tightened by rubber bands.

"Sure. Just spoke to Peter Lawford. We're glad you are going to sing. Anything great that puts Chicago on the map is mighty gratifying."

"We'll be glad to ride on your train, Mayor," Mahalia said.

"Congressman Dawson and John Johnson, the publisher of Ebony magazine, will be going with us, too," said the Mayor.

After the Mayor hung up, Mahalia called Mildred.

"Do you want to go to a party?" Mahalia asked.

"Sure," answered Mildred. "Whose party?"

"It's for the man who will be our next president," explained Mahalia, "John F. Kennedy. The party will be at the Armory in Washington and—"

"What?" shouted Mildred.

"And we're going with Mayor Daley in his special train and—"

"Mahalia," said Mildred, "what are you babbling about?"

"They want me to sing the national anthem at the President's inauguration party."

There was a long pause.

"Mildred, are you there?" Mahalia called into the phone.

"I'm here," said Mildred," but I can hardly believe what you've been telling me. Oh Mahalia, I'm so excited I think I'm going to cry!"

"I hope I can sing 'The Star Spangled Banner,' " Mahalia went on talking. "I've never sung it in public all by myself."

"We must practice, practice, practice," Mildred said.

And practice they did. Mahalia thought of little else.

Finally the day came to leave for Washington. The train was appointed like a luxury apartment. The passengers were fed fine food. The seats were deeply comfortable.

Mahalia thought of her first train ride, when she was just sixteen. She thought of the filth of that Jim Crow train and the box of food Aunt Duke had packed. And now here she was, riding with the Mayor of Chicago on her way to sing for the man who was to become president of the United States.

When Mahalia and Mildred went to the District of Columbia Armory, where the gala was to be held, the big place was full of people. Stagehands were hammering and sawing. Some people were stringing up flags and banners. Entertainers were rehearsing songs.

"Have you ever seen so many celebrities?" Mildred asked.

The place seemed swarming with comedians, singers, actors, musicians, some whom Mahalia and Mildred recognized. Many were busy with last minute rehearsing and planning.

"Is this really me?" Mahalia thought fleetingly. "The girl from New Orleans? And I'm going to help the nation celebrate its new president?"

Mahalia received instructions about her place on the program. Then she and Mildred went to their hotel room for a rest.

The gala was to begin at nine o'clock on Inauguration Eve. On this auspicious day, January 19, 1961, snow began to fall. By twilight the flakes were so thick a person could not see two feet ahead. Washington traffic was hampered. Cars and buses and streetcars were skidding into each other or getting stuck all over the city.

A taxi, creeping along at ten miles an hour, finally got Mahalia and Mildred to the Armory again. Nothing was going on. Entertainers were caught in snowdrifts all over town. Mahalia and Mildred sat at a table with some of the singers and dancers who had made it through. They were talking about the new First Lady and wondering how she would be accepted by the American people. They said she was aloof, artistic, and soft spoken. She'd been educated in boarding schools, Vassar College, and the Sorbonne. She'd studied history and languages and could speak fluently in French, Italian, and Spanish. Would the American public identify with her interests in art, antiques, fox hunting, horseback riding, and clothes?

Finally, about ten-thirty, conductor Leonard Bern-
stein led the seventy-piece orchestra in "Stars and
Stripes Forever" and then President Kennedy and his
family entered their box. The orchestra switched to
"Anchors Aweigh." The President looked lean and
fit. Mrs. Kennedy, wearing a lovely gown, smiled a
pixie-like smile and seemed engrossed by every detail
of the gala.

Everybody was standing up and applauding. From
the side entrances came all the famous actors,
actresses, singers, and dancers, as the orchestra
played, "Walking Down to Washington," which had
been especially written for the gala. Mahalia tingled
with the excitement of it all.

Then the lights dimmed. It was time for Mahalia
to sing. Mahalia stood alone on the stage. The glow
of the spotlight was on her. She shut her eyes and the
strains of the "Star Spangled Banner" began. She

sang the song in her spellbinding contralto voice, obviously deeply touched by every word she sang.

People clapped. Some remained standing. A glance at Mildred's face and Mahalia knew she had sung well. Mildred smiled and nodded vehemently.

The entertainment went on until almost two in the morning. At three o'clock, Mahalia felt drowsy and tired until she saw tall young man in a blue suit coming toward her. It was John F. Kennedy! He had come all the way across the Armory to give Mahalia a special thanks for opening the gala.

"Thank you, Miss Jackson," he said. "I've known your singing for a long time and have always admired it." He shook Mahalia's hand.

Later she told Mildred that he had a grip that made you feel his strength. "He looked into my eyes as if he was looking into my soul, and I realized how he was able to draw people to him in a magnetic way."

She had the same feelings about him the next morning when she sat in the bleachers in front of the Capitol to see the new president take the oath of office and to hear his inaugural address.

It was a bitter cold day, even with the sun shining. Heads were bowed in prayer when Mahalia noticed wisps of smoke curling from the lectern. Richard Cardinal Cushing was delivering the Inaugural invocation. He was not aware of smoke, but President Kennedy and Dwight D. Eisenhower, seated together near the smoking pulpit, did. A strong wind whipped the fumes into their faces, and they looked up from time to time.

A few seconds after Cardinal Cushing's "Amen," secret service agents squeezed down the aisle. They doused a smoldering electric motor used to adjust the lectern's height.

After Marian Anderson sang "The Star Spangled

Banner,'' Robert Frost, the distinguished poet, appeared before the microphones. His white hair was whisked about by the arctic wind. He began to read a verse he had written for the occasion. After the opening lines, he faltered, his 86-year-old eyes blinded by the reflection of brilliant sunshine flashing from the deep snow before him and the white marble behind.

"This," he told the tense crowd, "was to be the preface to a poem that I can say without reading."

Then in a pleasing baritone, he recited a poem he had written twenty years before, "The Gift Outright," changing the last line in honor of President Kennedy's "New Frontier."

But it was not the bitter cold, nor fire on the podium, nor the poet's dilemma that impressed Mahalia nearly as much as it was President Kennedy's inaugural speech. Certain phrases were deeply impressed in her mind.

"We observe today not a victory of party but a celebration of freedom. I have sworn before you and Almighty God the same solemn oath our forebears prescribed, the belief that rights of man come not from the generosity of the state but from the hand of God.

"If free society cannot help the many who are poor, it cannot save the few who are rich.

"—a struggle against the common enemies of man: tyranny, poverty, disease and war itself.

"And so, my fellow Americans, ask not what your country can do for you, ask what you can do for your country."

Mahalia turned to Mildred and said, "This man lifts my spirit and makes me feel part of the land I live in."

After the Inauguration, Mahalia and Mildred went on a concert tour that ran from New York to Texas. While on the road, Mahalia was getting mail about doing another tour of Europe. Mahalia said she would go if it could include the Holy Land. She had been singing all her life about Jesus' earthly home and she wanted to see the places she was singing about.

Europe and the Holy Land

Mahalia was glad to be sailing on the ship *United States*. Flowers and baskets of fruit were sent to her stateroom. But as the ship passed the Statue of Liberty, Mahalia gave in to her nervous exhaustion. The one-night stands during her tour had sapped her strength. It was the first time she had been on an ocean liner and she enjoyed looking at the sea and listening to the soothing sounds of the waves as they swept past the ship.

The first stop was England. The concert was at Albert Hall. Mahalia remembered that she had sung there in 1952. This time she had a feeling of victory, the Lord had brought her there and He was with her that night. She felt that she was singing to God and that the Lord's spirit was upon her.

She sang, "My Home Over There," a gospel song that reminded her of the Apostle Paul when he said, "I've fought the good fight and kept my faith."

Then she and Mildred whizzed through Belgium on the Trans-Europe Express until they got to Frankfurt, Germany, for a concert at the Kingresshalle. Then to Hamburg, which Mahalia called a crystal city because she bought crystal for her home in Chicago from some of the big and famous stores.

One day they took a Pan American plane and landed at the Copenhagen Airport where reporters swamped them with questions. They wanted to know if she had a hard time in America because of her color.

"I've had a hard time all my life," Mahalia told them. "Not just because of my color."

One reporter said, "I don't believe in God myself, but when you sing it gives me goose pimples."

"That's not goose pimples," Mahalia answered, "that's your soul speaking and you don't even know it's there!"

At Paris more reporters and photographers met them. In Zurich there was a dinner with the U.S. Consul General, Mr. Robert Peters.

Their route carried them by way of Italy and a visit at the Vatican. Mahalia joined a group in a huge room that was furnished with red chairs and red curtains and had a marble floor. Pope John XXIII walked in dressed in white robes. He spoke in French and a monsignor translated it for the group. He said it was important not to ignore the bad that is present in the world, but to labor to make the evil into godliness.

A train took them to Naples and they boarded a little Italian ship, *Esperial*, which was to sail across the Mediterranean Sea to the Middle East.

"Dear Lord," said Mahalia, "I'm going to walk in Jerusalem!"

It was a tiring journey, but Mahalia became excited as they came close to the place she wanted to see.

When she was younger she sang about Jerusalem.

> I'm going to walk in Jerusalem,
> Talk in Jerusalem,
> Shout in Jerusalem,
> Pray in Jerusalem,
> High up in Jerusalem
> When I die!

One morning, a soft and sunny morning, Mahalia and Mildred drove through the deep-cut hills of Galilee. Soon they reached the little town of Bethlehem. Guides took them into a stone courtyard and then into a big arched hall. Here was one of the world's oldest Christian churches standing on the site of the inn in which Mary and Joseph had sought lodging for the night.

Then Mahalia and Mildred went down a steep flight of stairs to a candle-lit chamber, where they saw the rock that is said to mark the spot where the manger was when Christ was born.

Mahalia thought, "It was near here that the first gospel singers sang. They were the angels. They sang of peace on earth and good will toward men, of joy to the world because our Savior had come. That's what gospel music is. It is an expression of joy and hope because God's Son came into the world."

Mahalia told Mildred, "That's the way the songs have always seemed to me all the years I've been singing them."

Later that day she and Mildred entered the walled garden of Gethsemane. The flowers sent out their fragrance. Silent monks from the old Church of St. Anne were tending the gardens. The two women saw the grove of olive trees, all twisted and gnarled. The guide said some of the olive trees were believed to be two thousand years old. Among these trees Jesus prayed and suffered as He knew that before morning He would be betrayed.

Then Mahalia and Mildred walked with their guide through the hot, narrow stone-cobbled streets of Old Jerusalem, filled with the sounds of crowds of people. People were crying out their wares just as they must have done for thousands of years since the times when men fought with spears.

Then they walked over the same path that the Lord had been taken along by Pontius Pilate's Roman soldiers. This was the route Jesus walked while bearing His cross.

Mahalia's sadness filled her whole being. Her heart beat faster; her throat tightened; her eyes welled with tears. "Oh, my Lord!" she murmured.

They came into a chapel in the Church of the Holy Sepulchre where the guide showed them a tiny marble chamber.

"Is this it?" Mahalia asked the guide.

"They believe this is the place," he answered quietly.

Mahalia knelt down and stayed there alone. She tried to find words for a prayer of thanks. Her dreams had come true. She had seen the place where Christ was born. She had touched the Rock of Calvary.

Later she told a group of friends, "In the old Hebrew of the Bible my name, Mahalia, means 'Blessed by the Lord,' and surely, it seemed to me, I had been blessed."

When Mahalia and Mildred returned to their hotel, reporters were waiting for them. "What message are you bringing to the Jews of Israel from America?" one reporter asked.

"I'm going to sing the same gospel songs I've always sung," Mahalia answered. "I'm not fixing to change my singing in Israel. I'm going to bring the Jews Christ."

The night Mahalia came on stage for her concert in Tel Aviv she wore a white gown and a necklace with a gold cross. Two thousand people (Muslims, Jews, and Christians) made up the audience.

Mahalia started her concert with "My Home Over There." Then she went on with "The Holy Bible," "Ain't Gonna Study War No More," and "Joshua Fit de Battle of Jericho."

Mahalia prayed that the audience would accept her. Her prayers were answered. When she completed the concert the audience shouted, "More! More! More!"

Mahalia came back and sang the Joshua song. There were more encores till the song she held for her last, "Mahalia's Not Gonna Sing No More."

Back in her room she fell on the bed, worn out by the concert tour and the emotional strain of her visit to the Holy Land.

"All my life I've been singing about the Holy Land," she murmured as Mildred plumped her pillows and drew a spread over her.

"Just think, Mildred," she said in a low, contemplative voice, "Jericho, the Dead Sea, Galilee, Bethlehem, Mount Hebron, Jerusalem, Calvary. I'm seeing it all as Jesus did! I walked in Jerusalem, talked in Jerusalem, shouted in Jerusalem, and prayed in Jerusalem. Thank You, Lord!"

She closed her eyes and dropped into a peaceful slumber.

She was ready to fly back to France and board the ship *United States*. On board ship on her way home, she enjoyed going over and over again in her mind the wonderful places she had visited in the Holy Land.

But the peaceful spirit she had enjoyed in the Holy Land disappeared when she heard the news in New York and Chicago. It was all about young people called the Freedom Riders. They had challenged the way the South was still treating black people in the intrastate bus terminals. The Supreme Court had ruled in 1958 that these places must not be segregated. But southerners were still forcing Negroes to use separate waiting rooms. "White" and "Colored" signs still appeared in the terminals' restaurants.

Later, when Mahalia was visiting in the South, she heard how a riot at the Montgomery, Alabama, bus terminal had touched off a great protest demonstration. Martin Luther King and Ralph Abernathy came up from Atlanta, Georgia, in May, 1961, for a special evening serivce at the First Baptist Church on Ripley Street in honor of the young Freedom Riders.

While the people sang, "Leaning on His Everlasting Arms," the Reverend King went down to the basement and telephoned Attorney General Robert Kennedy, who was standing by the telephones in Washington. "They are moving in on the church," King said. "Are you going to stop them?"

"We will stop them," Robert Kennedy answered.

On another telephone, Robert Kennedy was talking with the Governor of Alabama. A few minutes later the National Guard was ordered to the church. It took almost the rest of the night, but by dawn the soldiers had escorted the church people safely to their homes.

The big song of the movement that was being sung in the South by thousands of Negroes was "We Shall Overcome."

> We shall overcome, we shall overcome,
> We shall overcome some day.
> Deep in my heart I do believe
> We shall overcome some day.

Martin Luther King, Jr. said, "The Freedom Songs are giving the people new courage, a radiant hope in the future in our most trying hours."

Mahalia continued singing one-night-stand concerts in 1962—New York, Kansas City, Los Angeles, and Seattle. But she complained of being tired. She and Mildred went back to Chicago. She went into the hospital for tests where the doctors found she had diabetes and that her heart was strained. She was to stay in the hospital and rest. One night she slipped out of bed and dressed.

''Where in the world are you going?'' asked the attendant.

15

The March on Washington

"I am going home" announced Mahalia and left promptly.

She rested at home. She seldom left her home even to go to church. She called long distance to people like the Reverend Martin Luther King.

He asked her more than once, "When are you coming back down South where there is so much going on?"

"I can't come yet," she said in a voice that sounded happier than she felt.

But time passed and on a lovely summer day in August, 1963, she was in Washington, D.C., standing beside Dr. King on the steps of the Lincoln Memorial watching tens of thousands of people marching. Mahalia took a seat to listen to the speakers and to wait for her turn to sing.

She thought about how she was the granddaughter

of Negro slaves who had worked on a Louisiana plantation. All around her were great Negro leaders like Philip Randolph and Roy C. Wilkins and Martin Luther King and Whitney Young and John Lewis.

Dr. Ralph Bunche sat nearby. He had raised the American Negro to a new high in the United Nations. Thurgood Marshall, a federal judge who had won the famous Supreme Court decision in 1954, sat within speaking distance of Mahalia.

Mahalia waited for the signal to sing. Martin Luther King had given her the idea about which song to choose.

"Mahalia, why don't you sing 'I Been 'Bunked and I Been Scorned' for us?" he said.

Mahalia knew there were probably only a few white people who had ever heard that song, but it was an old spiritual that was known to black people up and down the land. It was exactly the right choice for this day because its words reflected the depth of feeling of all the Negroes who had come to Washington. It would reach all the millions who might be watching and listening on radio and TV.

When Mahalia stood to sing she sang the words softly.

> I been 'bunked and I been scorned.
> I'm gonna tell my Lord
> When I get home,
> Just how long you've been treating me wrong.

People were joining Mahalia in the singing. All through the great crowd hands were clapping and people who had been dipping their tired feet in the long reflection pool began to splash and rock to the rhythm.

She had scarcely finished when Dr. King was up to the podium. He delivered a speech which was to make him famous.

"I have a dream," he cried out, "that one day on the red hills of Georgia the sons of former slaves and sons of former slave owners will be able to sit down together at the table of brotherhood.

"I have a dream that my four little children will one day live in a nation where they will not be judged by the color of their skin but by the content of their character.

"I have a dream that one day little black boys and little black girls will be able to join hands with little white boys and white girls and walk together as sisters and brothers."

It was the greatest speech of the day. Over at the White House, President Kennedy congratulated the leaders on the way the march had gone. President Kennedy was appreciated by Negros. He had done much to make the Negro feel that the United States belonged to him as much as to any white person.

Mahalia was in California on November 22, 1963, leaving for a television show rehearsal, when Mildred Falls came running to her, shouting, ''They just said on the radio that President Kennedy has been shot!''

Numbly they got into the car. They started for the TV studio, saying over and over again to each other, ''It can't be. It must be a mistake.'' When they got to the TV studio people were crying. Some were wringing their hands.

''He's dead!'' someone said.

Mahalia cried out, ''Oh, no, Jesus!''

She insisted upon going back to her hotel room where she knelt beside her bed. All the memories of the many times she had seen him and listened to him talk, since the first time she had noticed him as a young senator at the Chicago Convention in 1952, came flooding back to her. Everything he had said and done to help people came into Mahalia's mind.

The news accounts on the TV kept on giving the impressions of some people. Commentators commented. The nation was torn with grief. Mahalia listened and watched through misty eyes.

On TV she saw Love Field in Dallas. There was hardly a cloud in the sky. A crowd of several thousand people pressed against the fence. There were many signs speaking of welcome and support.

The newsreel showed the presidential plane landing and the plane door opening. President Kennedy came out and walked down the ramp. Dallas Mayor Earle Cabell headed the greeting committee. Someone gave Jacqueline Kennedy a bouquet of red roses.

She was 34, a beautiful wife, young mother, a good athlete. She had surprised the nation by making more changes in the White House than did all the First Ladies who came before her. The restoration of the White House generated so much interest and national pride that eight hundred thousand people toured the mansion the first six months after the restoration.

"Lots of people were wrong about her," mused Mahalia. "She's a fine First Lady!" Mahalia reached for another handkerchief to dry her tears.

Mahalia's attention was again drawn to the TV screen which showed the motorcade headed downtown.

At Lemmon Avenue and Lomo Street a group of school girls waved a sign: "Mr. President, Please Stop and Shake our Hands." The President grinned, the convertible halted, the girls giggled, rushed forward, and clutched at his outstretched hand.

In Dallas, the big clock on the Mercantile National Bank ticked past noon. The motorcade turned off Main Street and had only to make one final turn in front of that big building up ahead. The building was the Texas Book Depository Building. The crowd craned for a last look as the motorcade made the turn and headed for the freeway.

The president probably never heard the shot or knew what hit him. It was a piece of metal a little thinner than an ordinary pencil. It struck him in the back, penetrating two or three inches. He was struck as he turned to wave. His hands snapped up reflexively to his throat. Wordlessly, he slumped over toward his wife, who was sitting on his left in the back seat.

In the jump seat ahead, Governor John Connally turned and a second bullet caught him in the back, passed through, struck his right wrist, and lodged in his thigh. The third and last shot hit the back of the president's head about ear-level, as he bowed forward.

Mrs. Kennedy cried out, in the first instant of horror, "Oh, my God, they killed my husband! Jack! Jack!"

"I can't watch anymore," Mahalia sobbed.

Later she learned that the sniper who killed President Kennedy had been jailed. His name was Lee Harvey Oswald.

President Kennedy's sad death filled Mahalia's thoughts. A tall, soft-spoken man named Sigmund Galloway tried to comfort her. He was living in California where Mahalia was making recordings and singing in concerts.

Mahalia had known Sigmund Galloway's family through the Baptist Church for many years. They lived in Gary, Indiana, where Mahalia went to sing.

Sigmund liked music. Sometimes he played in an orchestra and he did some arranging.

At this time Mahalia knew all about the joys of a successful career, but she also knew how empty and lonely life could be when coming home from big tours to her house in Chicago. Although she had friends all over the United States and Europe, she was alone a lot of the time.

About two months after her return from a European tour, Sigmund Galloway asked her to marry him. She accepted. She and Sigmund were married in her living room by the Reverend Leon Jenkins, pastor of the Greater Salem Baptist Church. A few friends were invited. Mahalia looked forward to an even happier and more fulfilled life.

Mahalia continued to sing, and she gave more and more of her time to helping Martin Luther King. In 1966 she appeared with him at Soldiers' Field in Chicago before an audience of over fifty thousand people. At another King meeting, she not only sang but also paid the rent for the building where he spoke.

The songs people liked at this time were Freedom songs. Many of them were spirituals that slaves had sung as they hoped and prayed for a better life. Some had new words set to the music of the old hymns.

Then, on April 4, 1968, Mahalia was crushed by sorrow again.

The report came over the TV that as Dr. Martin Luther King left his motel room to go to dinner, he paused to lean over the balcony to talk to some friends in the courtyard below. Across the street, an assassin took aim and blasted away. Martin Luther King, eyes wide open, lay on the floor of the balcony, bleeding from a huge neck wound. In minutes he was dead.

Across the street, James Earl Ray dropped his rifle and ran. Two months later Ray, an ex-convict, was captured by the FBI. He was eventually convicted of this crime. Ray claimed at his trial that he was a hired killer. He said he was a part of a conspiracy.

More than fifty thousand people marched in Martin Luther King, Jr.'s funeral procession through Atlanta on April 9, 1968.

This was a sorrow that seemed almost too much for Mahalia to bear. She was asked to sing at the funeral in Atlanta, Georgia. She said she would.

To Mildred she said, "I don't know if I can do it. It will be the hardest thing I'll ever have to do in my whole life."

Mahalia did control herself and the tears that welled up were like ever-flowing fountains.

Mahalia sang "Precious Lord, Take My Hand." Everyone said she sang it beautifully. The tears spilled over and a mourning crowd wept with her. Television cameras filmed the funeral. Mahalia's song went into thousands of homes. People said it expressed the great sense of loss they were feeling.

Carved into the tombstone on King's grave are the words "Free at Last!"

But Mahalia said that Dr. King was always free because he believed in himself and others, and because he was not afraid to stand up for what he thought was right.

"He had this way," said Mahalia, "of giving people the feeling they could be bigger and stronger and more courageous and more loving than they thought they could be."

Editorials of the time agreed with Mahalia. They said the gentle spiritual leader left a great lesson to the world. You can protest without hating. You can struggle without violence. Love will outlast hate.

One writer wrote, "Dreamers die, but dreams pass on. Dreams and ideas know no boundaries of race or time or place. Thoreau passed his ideas to Gandhi, who passed them along to an American dreamer named Martin Luther King. Dr. King wove the ideas into a dream for a better world—a world where all men might live in peace and love, without poverty" (Lillie Patterson).

Mahalia went back to Chicago, her heart sad. But as usual when she was unhappy or in trouble, she kept busy with her singing. She gave more concerts.

There was a concert in a Harlem park in July, 1969. Some twenty thousand blacks and whites stood, waiting for Mahalia to sing. This was another one of the free concerts for the public during the hot days when rioting was expected.

It had rained earlier that day. But the sweltering heat had returned. Still the crowd waited.

As Mahalia prepared to sing, she remembered that the blacks sang in Africa to make the soil right for planting. They sang to make the harvest plentiful. They sang when horrible slave ships brought them in chains across the Atlantic Ocean.

Mahalia knew the sadness of those songs when the black man, even after Emancipation, found himself still on the outside of freedom. He found he was not free to vote, hold office, and or receive the white man's justice in the courts.

The songs were passed down from one generation to another. Mahalia had been listening to them almost from the day she was born. She never let anyone change their truth. She remembered God through all the sorrow.

Mahalia was ready for the concert in Harlem. The heat was almost unbearable. Storm clouds threatened up above. Mahalia began singing "Just a Closer Walk with Thee." As she sang she was remembering Rosa Parks; she was remembering how her people marched through snarling dogs, through tear gas and baseball bats wielded by bigots.

Mahalia's next song was "Take My Hand, Precious Lord." This had been Martin Luther King's favorite. Tears came into Mahalia's eyes. Some people in the audience began to weep aloud for their fallen leader.

Tears streamed down Mahalia's cheeks. She was crying for Dr. King and others like Medgar Evers, for President Kennedy and his brother Robert. She cried for Malcolm X, for Schwerner and Goodman and Cheney (murdered in Mississippi), and for Mrs. Liuzzo and so many, many others.

People were always asking Mahalia to perform. But her work did not seem to give her the pleasure it once had. Her marriage to Sigmund tragically ended in divorce. Her brother Peter was dead; Aunt Duke was dead; Mahalia felt tired and alone.

But in 1971, when she was sixty, the government asked her to fly to an American outpost in Japan to sing for the soldiers. She accepted. Her doctors warned her against such trips.

"Just this last time," Mahalia said.

When Mahalia returned from Japan, they had another chore for her. This time it was Germany. There was trouble between the black and white

American troops stationed there. Officials thought that Mahalia's gospel songs would be a healing factor between the two races. That Thanksgiving, 1971, she was at an army outpost in Germany. Spectators said she sang songs with special tenderness and reverence. The men loved her.

Then she collapsed on the stage and was rushed to an Army hospital, seriously ill. The doctors wanted to keep her there until she was strong enough to return to America.

Mahalia shook her head "No." She thought she could recover much better back home.

Mahalia was brought to Little Company of Mary Hospital in a Chicago suburb. Hospital switchboards were busy day and night as people called to find out how Mahalia was getting along. Flowers from friends and strangers banked her room.

On Thursday, January 27, 1972, Mahalia died. The news spread quickly through the city. The news was flashed across the nation.

Thousands of people mourned.

EPILOGUE

A bitterly cold wind whipped Chicago on that January day when lines formed outside the Greater Salem Baptist Church. Fifty thousand people who had known Mahalia Jackson filed past her mahogany coffin in a final tribute to one of the greatest gospel singers the world has ever known

The next day, as many as could—six thousand or more—filled every seat and stood along the walls of the city's public concert hall, the Arie Crown Theater of McCormick Place, for a two-hour long funeral service.

It was not a funeral service dedicated to grief. There were joyous songs and eulogies. After all, many said, Mahalia's talent brought happiness, not tears.

Three days later, over a thousand miles away, there was a similar scene. Long lines and thousands of people filled the great hall of the Rivergate Convention Center in downtown New Orleans.

In Chicago, the plain people and famous people like Mayor Richard J. Daley, Aretha Franklin, Coretta King, Sammy Davis, and Ella Fitzgerald had paid their respects.

In New Orleans, Mayor Moon Landrieu and Louisiana Governor John J. McKeithen joined with the poor blacks from Mahalia's old neighborhood.

When the funeral cortege drove slowly past her childhood church, Mt. Moriah Baptist Church, her recordings played through loudspeakers.

When she was buried, outside of New Orleans, a message from President Nixon read, "Millions of ears will miss the sound of the great, rich voice making a joyful noise unto the Lord."

SONGS MAHALIA LOVED

IT'S ME

Refrain:
>   It's me, it's me, it's me, O Lord,
>   Standin' in de need of pray'r.
>   It's me, it's me, it's me, O Lord,
>   Standin' in de need of pray'r.

1.   Not my brother, not my sister,
>   but it's me, O Lord,
>   Standin' in de need of pray'r.
>   Not my brother, not my sister,
>   but it's me, O Lord,
>   Standin' in de need of pray'r.

2.   Not my mother, not my father,
>   But it's me, O Lord . . . .

3.   Not the preacher, not the deacon,
>   But it's me, O Lord . . . .

OH, DIDN'T IT RAIN

Forty days, forty nights when de rain kept a fallin',
De wicked clumb de tree, an' for help kept a callin',
For they heard de waters wailin'
>   Didn't it rain, rain, didn't it rain,
>   Tell me, Noah, didn't it rain?

Some clim'd de mountain, some clim'd de hill,
Some started sailin' and a-rowin' wid a will'
Some tried swimmin' and I guess
>   they're swimmin' still,
For they heard de waters roarin'
>   Didn't it rain, rain, didn't it rain,
>   Tell me, Noah, didn't it rain?

MOVIN' ON UP

Move on up a little higher;
Meet with Paul and Silas.

Move on up a little higher;
Meet the Lily of the Valley.

> (*With verses like these, Mahalia often kept the audience
> excited for a half hour or so.*)

WALK TOGETHER CHILDREN

1. O walk together children,
      don't you get weary.
    (*Repeat two more times.*)
    There's a great camp meeting
      in the Promised Land.

2. O talk together children . . . .

Refrain:
      Going to mourn and never tire,
      Mourn and never tire,
      Mourn and never tire,
      There's a great camp meeting
        in the Promised Land.

3. O get you ready children . . . .

4. For Jesus is a-coming . . . .

5. O I feel the spirit moving . . . .

6. O now I'm getting happy . . . .

Refrain:
      Going to shout and never tire,
      Shout and never tire,
      Shout and never tire,
      There's a great camp meeting
        in the Promised Land.

SOMETIMES I FEEL LIKE
A MOTHERLESS CHILE

1.   Sometimes I feel like a motherless chile,
     Sometimes I feel like a motherless chile,
     Sometimes I feel like a motherless chile,
     Far, far away from home;
         a long, long ways from home.

Refrain:
     Then I get down on my knees an' pray,
     Get down on my knees an' pray.

2.   Sometimes I feel like I'm almost gone . . . .

AIN'T GONNA STUDY WAR NO MORE

1.   I'm gonna lay down my burden
     Down by the riverside,
     Down by the riverside,
     Down by the riverside,
     I'm gonna lay down my burden
     Down by the riverside.
     Ain't gonna study war no more.

Refrain:
     Ain't gonna study war no more.
         (*Repeat five more times*).

2.   I'm gonna lay down my sword and shield . . . .

3.   I'm gonna put on my long white robe . . . .

4.   I'm gonna talk with the Prince of Peace . . . .

PRECIOUS LORD, TAKE MY HAND

Precious Lord, take my hand,
   lead me on, let me stand,
I am tired, I am weary, and I want,
Through the storm, through the night,
   lead me on to the light.
Take my hand, precious Lord, and lead me on.
Precious Lord, take my hand,
   lead me on, only let me stand.
Oh I'm tired, Oh I'm weary, and I want.
Through the storm, through the night,
   lead me on a-to the light.
You take my hand, precious Lord,
   and lead me on, on and on.

THE LORD'S PRAYER

Our Father, which art in Heaven,
   Hallowed a-be Thy name;
Thy Kingdom come, Thy will be done,
   Hallowed a-be Thy name;
On the earth as it is in Heaven,
   Hallowed a-be Thy name;
Give us this day our daily bread,
   Hallowed a-be Thy name;
And forgive us all our trespasses.
   Hallowed a-be Thy name;
As we forgive those who trespass against us,
   Hallowed a-be Thy name;
And lead us not to the Devil to be tempted,
   Hallowed a-be Thy name;
But deliver us from all that is evil,
   Hallowed a-be Thy name;
For Thine is the Kingdom, the power and the glory,
   Hallowed a-be Thy name;
For ever, for ever, and for ever and ever,
   Hallowed a-be Thy name.
Amen, Amen, Amen, Amen,
   Hallowed a-be Thy name;
Amen, Amen, Amen, Amen,
   Hallowed a-be Thy name.

BIBLIOGRAPHY

Notable Illinois Women by Collins and Witter. Quest Publishing, Rock Island, Illinois.

Political Profiles (Abernathy).

Mahalia Jackson . . . Queen of Gospel Song by Jean Gay Cornell. Garrard Publishing Co. 1974.

Famous Negro Music Makers by Langston Hughes. Dodd, Mead & Company 1955.

Make a Joyful Noise Unto The Lord! by Jesse Jackson. Thomas Y. Crowell Company 1974.

Martin Luther King, Jr. Man of Peace by Lillie Patterson. Garrard Publishing Company 1969.

Martin Luther King, Jr. by Jacqueline L. Harris. Franklin Watts 1983.

Mahalia Jackson by Evan McLeod Wylie. Hawthorn Books, Inc. 1966.

Big Star Fallin' Mama by Hettie Jones. The Viking Press 1974.

"The Torch Is Passed," The Associated Press Story of the Death of a President.

"Ebony Magazine," April 1972.

"Ebony Magazine," March 1972.

"The Saturday Evening Post," December 1959.

"Ladies Home Journal," November 1963.

INDEX

ABOUT THE AUTHOR

Evelyn Witter, English teacher, was once assigned by the school principal to teach a creative writing class. "We don't have a textbook," he said, "but I'm sure you can get along without one." And she did. She enjoys helping young people learn how to write. Mrs. Witter, who lives in Illinois, wrote the Sower Series book, *Abigail Adams.*

ABOUT THE ARTIST

Jan Jones lives in Michigan and enjoys drawing people—all kinds of people. She admires Mahalia Jackson and was eager to illustrate a book about this great singer.

SOWERS SERIES

ATHLETE
Billy Sunday, Home Run to Heaven
   by Robert Allen

EXPLORERS AND PIONEERS
Christopher Columbus, Adventurer of Faith and Courage
   by Bennie Rhodes
Johnny Appleseed, God's Faithful Planter, John Chapman
   by David Collins

HOMEMAKERS
Abigail Adams, First Lady of Faith and Courage
   by Evelyn Witter
Susanna Wesley, Mother of John and Charles
   by Charles Ludwig

HUMANITARIANS
Jane Addams, Founder of Hull House
   by David Collins
Florence Nightingale, God's Servant at the Battlefield
   by David Collins
Teresa of Calcutta, Serving the Poorest of the Poor
   by D. Jeanene Watson
Clara Barton, God's Soldier of Mercy
   by David Collins

MUSICIANS AND POETS
Francis Scott Key, God's Courageous Composer
   by David Collins
Samuel Francis Smith, My Country, 'Tis of Thee
   by Marguerite E. Fitch